COMMONSENSE QUESTIONS
ABOUT INSTRUCTION

Other Titles by Gerard Giordano

Capping Costs: Putting a Price Tag on School Reform (2012)

Teachers Go to Rehab: Historical and Current Advice to Instructors (2012)

Lopsided Schools: Case Method Briefings (2011)

Cockeyed Education: A Case Method Primer (2010)

Solving Education's Problems Effectively: A Guide to Using the Case Method (2009)

COMMONSENSE QUESTIONS ABOUT INSTRUCTION

The Answers Can Provide
Essential Steps to Improvement

Gerard Giordano

ROWMAN & LITTLEFIELD EDUCATION
A DIVISION OF

ROWMAN & LITTLEFIELD
Lanham • Boulder • New York • Toronto • Plymouth, UK

Published by Rowman & Littlefield Education
A division of Rowman & Littlefield
4501 Forbes Boulevard, Suite 200, Lanham, Maryland 20706
www.rowman.com

10 Thornbury Road, Plymouth PL6 7PP, United Kingdom

British Library Cataloguing in Publication Information Available

Library of Congress Cataloging-in-Publication Data

Library of Congress Cataloging-in-Publication Data Available

ISBN 978-1-4758-0508-6 (cloth : alk. paper)—ISBN 978-1-4758-0509-3
(pbk. : alk. paper)—ISBN 978-1-4758-0510-9 (electronic)

♾™ The paper used in this publication meets the minimum requirements of
American National Standard for Information Sciences—Permanence of Paper
for Printed Library Materials, ANSI/NISO Z39.48-1992.

Printed in the United States of America

This book is for my incomparable students.

CONTENTS

PREFACE
HAVE COMMONSENSE
QUESTIONS AFFECTED TEACHING?

What is the most important subject?

—"What Is the Most," 2007

What makes a great teacher?

—Amanda Ripley, 2010

Discipline in school: what works and what doesn't?

—Sherry Bowen, 2010

On what should politicians base their decisions?

—Michael De Dora, 2010

Should we be paying students?

—"Should We Be," 2011

What is the best way to teach children to read?

—National Institutes of Health, 2012

What should children read?

—Sara Mosle, 2012

Should schools continue to use textbooks?

—"Should Schools Continue," 2012

Is your child happy in school?

—"Is Your Child," 2012

What makes a great school?

—Sam Chaltain, 2012

Is it right for parents to take over schools?

—Randy Speck, 2012

[Are] iPads in school . . . a toy or a tool?

—Steve Lopez, 2013

Should students influence how much teachers get paid?

—"Should Students Influence," 2013

What is the purpose of school?

—Stephanie Rivera, 2013

Baseball fans wanted to know about talented players. They especially wanted to know about emerging stars, such as the rookie Bryce Harper.

Harper stood out from other baseball rookies. He was remarkably athletic, personable, articulate, nineteen years old, and a member of the Church of Jesus Christ of Latter-Day Saints.

Harper played several times in Toronto during 2012. He was the center of attention after hitting a towering home run in one of those games.

The Toronto reporters were eager to pose questions at the postgame news conference. One of them asked Harper whether he intended to celebrate by going out on the town for drinks. He explained that Harper would be able to purchase alcohol in Canada because it had a lower legal drinking age than the United States.

Harper understood that the reporter was not asking a sincere question. He realized that he wished to make him feel uncomfortable about his church, which discouraged alcohol.

Harper responded curtly to the reporter: he stated that he would not be answering any *clown questions* ("Bryce Harper's Retort," 2012).

        ◦   ◦   ◦   ◦   ◦

Parents wanted to know about the schools. They especially wanted to know about the instruction that their children received in them.

The parents posed questions about a full range of instructional topics. They directed them to the teachers.

- What is instruction's goal?
- What are the fundamental subjects?
- What prods learning?
- How complex is classroom discipline?
- What are the right questions about textbooks?
- How much technology do teachers need?
- Do grades matter?
- What prods politicians to collaborate on schools?
- How much data about teachers is needed?

The parents expected teachers to answer their questions. They were struck by the many who were silent.

Parents realized that the teachers did not answer some questions because they were difficult. They suspected that they did not answer others because they made them feel uncomfortable.

The parents were annoyed at the unresponsive teachers; they wished to put pressure on them. At the same time, they realized that the teachers were protected by powerful allies. They resolved to recruit their own allies.

        ◦   ◦   ◦   ◦   ◦

This book examines commonsense questions about the schools. It is written in an engaging style, has a distinctive point of view, and is filled with engrossing examples.

Stimulating comments are placed at the beginning of each chapter. They encapsulate key points from the current dialogue about instruction. Those at the beginning of this section set the tone for the entire book.

This book is intended for the professionals who work directly in the schools: teachers, administrators, and guidance counselors. It also is intended for the persons who interact with schools indirectly: professors, politicians, school board members, parents, and the general public.

Case method activities are placed in every chapter. These can be completed by individual readers. They also can be completed by the participants in case-based seminars.

The case method activities help readers examine commonsense questions about instruction. They also help them identify the groups that posed the questions, their motives, the persons to whom they directed them, and the influence that they had on teaching.

This book is the first in a series. The next book will examine commonsense questions directed to school administrators. It will look at personnel, salaries, accountability, teacher incentives, facilities, scheduling, budgets, marketing, and political influences.

Another volume will focus on testing. It will examine the questions about assessment from parents, employers, and politicians. Still another volume will focus on school ethics. It will examine questions about race, gender, disability, income, and religion.

ACKNOWLEDGMENT

I cannot overstate how much I value, depend on, and appreciate my extraordinary editor, Tom Koerner.

1

WHY ASK SHREWD QUESTIONS?

School leaders and staff must be engaged in curricular issues beyond
. . . boilerplate.

—Leo Bradley, 2004

The boilerplate [answer] . . . includes getting more school money
into classrooms.

—Ross Ramsey, 2012

[The politician] stuck . . . to his boilerplate.

—Daniel Ward, 2013

Boilerplate . . . pervades all aspects of our modern lives.

—Margaret Radin, 2013

Politicians confronted shrewdly crafted questions. They devised
strategies to deal with them. They made an enormous impression on
educators.

POLITICAL QUESTIONS AND ANSWERS

Politicians were nonplussed by difficult-to-answer questions. They noted that many of the most difficult questions were coming from journalists.

Questions

John Edwards was an affluent politician. He secured the Democratic Party's nomination for vice president in 2004. He was disappointed when he lost the election.

Edwards was ready to try for national office again in 2008. This time, he hoped to become president.

Edwards searched for a way to differentiate himself from the other presidential candidates. He decided to campaign on a pledge to help low-income families.

Journalists doubted whether the wealthy Edwards truly empathized with poor Americans. They were eager to challenge him.

Some of the journalists uncovered an incident in which Edwards had spent twelve-hundred dollars for a haircut. They asked him how he could reconcile this sort of spending with his pledge to help impoverished Americans ("Cost of Edwards' Haircut," 2009).

The journalists unmercifully harassed Edwards with haircut questions. In spite of their persistence, few were surprised when he refused to respond ("John Edwards Reduced," 2012; Rubin, 2012a).

Journalists lost interest in Edwards for a time after the 2008 election. They became curious about him once more after he was accused of illicit campaign spending. They began to badger him anew with haircut questions (Petri, 2012).

Answers

Politicians realized that journalists did not expect answers to all of their questions. Nonetheless, they were concerned about the way they would be perceived if they were silent. They feared that the public would think less of them. They asked media advisors for help.

Boilerplate Media advisors were eager to help the politicians. They recommended a strategy from business: they directed them to employ *boilerplate*.

The advisors explained that business professionals relied extensively on boilerplate. They gave examples of lawyers who used it to draft contracts, marketing personnel who used it to construct prospectuses, and technology experts who used it to create websites (Cordero-Moss, 2011; Dunlap, 1990; Manian, 2012; Radin, 2013).

The advisors encouraged politicians to prepare boilerplate on domestic and foreign issues. They explained that they could rely on it when they faced disconcerting questions (Howard, 2006; Kalb, Peters, & Woolley, 2007; Luntz, 2007).

The advisors were certain that boilerplate would be effective with persistent journalists. They warned that it would be so effective that it could antagonize them (Cornog, 2004; Lim, 2008).

Mitt Romney was the Republican presidential candidate in 2012. He was pressed by journalists to give precise reasons why voters should choose him. He infuriated them when he responded with political boilerplate. Nonetheless, they conceded that most members of the public tolerated it without complaining (Goodman, 2012).

Barack Obama, the Democratic candidate, also was pressed to identify the reasons that voters should give him another term in office. Although he incensed journalists when he resorted to boilerplate, he did not perturb members of the public (Cary, 2012; Henninger, 2012; Knoller, 2012; Noah, 2012; Rubin, 2012b; "Transformers 2," 2012).

Prescreening Journalists were vexed when politicians used boilerplate. They became especially annoyed when they used the boilerplate from one topic to address questions on unrelated topics. They noted that they were using economics boilerplate to respond to questions about defense (Charteris-Black, 2005; Giordano, 2012a).

The journalists looked for opportunities to catch politicians off-guard. They fired questions at them as they passed through crowds. Because they were sequestered behind rope cordons, they referred to these queries as *ropeline questions* (Todd, Murray, Brower, & Cucchiara, 2012).

Politicians were unprepared for ropeline questions. Some of them ignored them; others responded with boilerplate. Still others experimented with prescreening.

Politicians directed the journalists to submit all queries for pre-screening. They then would have the time they needed to carefully deliberate about responses. They warned that any journalists who did not comply would be denied private interviews. They were disappointed when most of the journalists disregarded their directive and threat (Peters, 2012).

EDUCATIONAL INQUIRY

Parents had questions about schools. They focused many of them on instruction.

Teachers

Parents noted that teachers were using the same instructional techniques that their predecessors had used generations ago. They asked them why they were not relying on newer techniques (Giordano, 2009).

The parents assumed that the teachers would answer them. They were upset when many did not. They judged that some were stumped. They judged that others viewed the parents as intruders in a domain where they did not belong.

The parents wished to put pressure on the uncooperative teachers. They looked for allies to assist them. They decided that allies from business would be invaluable.

Questions Some businesspeople were ready to confront uncooperative teachers. Like the parents, they posed questions directly to teachers. Like them, they expected answers.

The businesspeople were furious when teachers did not answer their questions. They realized that they might be ignoring questions that were difficult to answer or intrusive. They judged that they also were ignoring those that made them uncomfortable.

Even though the businesspeople were irate, they discovered that it was difficult for them to place pressure on teachers. They realized that they had special job protections. They tried to demonstrate that the protections were unreasonable (Giordano, 2011; Zernike, 2012).

Answers   Businesspeople asked the public school teachers why they needed special job protections. They pointed out that the teachers hired by for-profit schools did not have them.

Businesspeople already had asked this question to the professors at public universities. They had asked why they needed more job protections than peers at for-profit universities.

The professors had countered with a question of their own. They asked the businesspeople why for-profit universities assigned a higher priority to corporate revenue than student learning (Giordano, 2012a).

The teachers were impressed by the clever way in which the professors had used their own question to deflect the original question. They decided to copy them: they asked businesspeople why for-profit schools were more concerned about earning than learning (Boyles, 2005; Weil, 2002).

The teachers were heartened when federal politicians joined the debate between the professors and their critics. They applauded when the politicians accused for-profit universities of unprofessional and unethical practices. They hoped that they would censure for-profit schools as well (Fabricant & Fine, 2012; Gammeltoft & McCormick, 2010; Lewin, 2012).

School Administrators

Although many businesspeople strongly supported public school teachers, others were angry at them. In fact, they were angry at the school administrators as well. They scolded the administrators for allowing teachers to become unruly.

Questions   The irate businesspeople threatened to replace the traditional public school administrators with entrepreneurial leaders, such as those who managed the for-profit schools. They claimed that these leaders had done better at increasing worker productivity and reducing operating budgets. They noted that they also had created profits for their firms (Giordano, 2012a; Young, 2012).

Irate businesspeople repeatedly asked public school administrators whether they were evolving into leaders similar to those at the for-profit schools. They were displeased when they did not respond.

Answers   The school administrators assumed that the irate businesspeople were using shrewd questions to make them feel uncomfortable. Nonetheless, they felt pressure to answer them.

The school administrators were impressed by the manner in which politicians had used boilerplate to answer questions from journalists. They decided that they would employ it to answer questions from angry businesspeople.

The school administrators had an almost inexhaustible supply of information about instructional leadership. They conceded that little of it addressed the queries from the businesspeople. Nonetheless, they resolved that they would fashion it into boilerplate. Some of them even used this term to characterize it. They were ready to adduce it when they were challenged by difficult questions (Bradley, 2004; Strauss, 2012; Toppo, 2012).

Just as politicians had not expected boilerplate to satisfy journalists, the school administrators did not expect it to satisfy angry businesspeople. However, they hoped that it created the appearance that they were responding to questions. They hoped that it made a positive impression not on businesspeople but rather on members of the public and parents with children in the public schools.

The administrators in a Florida school district had to deal with hard questions about their Virtual Instruction Academy, which encompassed a set of state-funded online courses. They responded with a boilerplate statement about the courses.

[The Virtual Instruction Academy creates] an environment of acceptance, developing an alliance of all stakeholders, and expanding learning to an individualized adventure utilizing innovative solutions . . . [and can be referred to as] Virtual Education, Cyber Education, On-line Education, E-Learning, Mobile Learning, and Distance Learning. . . . Virtual education is best described as a learning opportunity where the student and the educator are separate from one another by space, time, and often both . . . [and] can include but are not limited to: multimedia resources, internet, video conferencing, webinars, simulations, and other alternatives. . . . Asynchronous learning occurs when the student and educator work on their own time and pace, but most often within a framework schedule . . . [while] synchronous learning occurs when the educator and student are in the learning environment at the same time . . . [and] virtual education can contain both asynchronous and synchronous opportunities of learning and instruction. (Duval County Public Schools, 2010)

One journalist constructed a patently meaningless statement. He wrote that "aligned instruction with buy-in by highly qualified teachers for authentic inquiry-based learning and student engagement in professional learning communities will produce 21st century skills." He waggishly asked whether this piece of boilerplate was substantively different from those that educators had been supplying (Merrow, 2011).

CASE METHOD

The case method is relatively new in educator preparation. Nonetheless, it has been used for decades in other fields. It has been used for over a century to prepare lawyers.

Professors of law introduced their students to the case method in university seminars. They required them to use it for academic problems; they hoped that they later would use it to solve courtroom problems.

Education professors were impressed by the case method. They encouraged aspiring teachers to use it in college lecture halls. They hoped that they later would use it to solve problems in public and private schools (Giordano, 2009, 2010, 2011, 2012).

Case method activities fill this book. They are placed at the end of each chapter. They could be appropriate for professional educators who are enrolled in seminars. However, they are intended for individual readers.

By following the cues in the activities, readers simulate the investigative processes in case-based seminars. Like the participants in those seminars, they draw their own conclusions about the reasons that important educational questions were posed and the ways that groups responded to them.

The following set of case method activities focuses on shrewd questions. It explores the ways in which persons responded to them.

EXAMINING SHREWD QUESTIONS AND ANSWERS

Politicians used special techniques to handle shrewd questions. They made an impression on educators.

Activity 1.1

Republican politicians had to deal with shrewd questions about foreign and domestic issues. They sometimes gave boilerplate answers. How did groups respond?

Table 1.1 identifies two groups: journalists and members of the public.

Complete the table by indicating the ways in which groups responded to boilerplate answers from the Republican politicians. You can use symbols.

Use the symbol – if groups exhibited low interest. Use the symbol ± for moderate interest and the symbol + for high interest. As a final step, explain the bases for the symbols that you selected.

You can rely on the information in this chapter, additional information, or the information cited in the references. If you are reading this chapter with colleagues, you can confer with them.

Table 1.1.　Republican Politicians Use Boilerplate

Groups	Response*	Explanation
Journalists		
Members of the Public		

*– Low
 ± Moderate
 + High

Activity 1.2

Democratic politicians had to deal with shrewd questions about foreign and domestic issues. They sometimes gave boilerplate answers. How did groups respond?

Table 1.2 identifies two groups: journalists and members of the public.

Complete the table by indicating the ways in which groups responded to boilerplate answers from the Democratic politicians. You can use symbols.

Use the symbol – if groups exhibited low interest. Use the symbol ± for moderate interest and the symbol + for high interest. As a final step, explain the bases for the symbols that you selected.

Table 1.2. Democratic Politicians Use Boilerplate

Groups	Response*	Explanation
Journalists		
Members of the Public		

*– Low
± Moderate
+ High

Activity 1.3

Public school teachers had to deal with shrewd questions about their special job protections. They sometimes posed counterquestions. How did groups respond?

Table 1.3 identifies two groups: businesspeople who prized for-profit schools and politicians who criticized for-profit universities.

Complete the table by indicating the ways in which groups responded to counterquestions from public school teachers. You can use symbols.

Use the symbol – if groups exhibited low interest. Use the symbol ± for moderate interest and the symbol + for high interest. As a final step, explain the bases for the symbols that you selected.

Table 1.3.   Public School Teachers Use Counterquestions

Groups	Response*	Explanation
Businesspeople—Prize For-Profit Schools		
Politicians—Criticize For-Profit Universities		

*– Low
 ± Moderate
 + High

Activity 1.4

Public school administrators had to deal with shrewd questions about their leadership. They sometimes gave boilerplate answers. How did groups respond?

Table 1.4 identifies two groups: businesspeople who prized for-profit schools and parents of children in the public schools.

Complete the table by indicating the ways in which groups responded to boilerplate answers from the public school administrators. You can use symbols.

Use the symbol – if groups exhibited low interest. Use the symbol ± for moderate interest and the symbol + for high interest. As a final step, explain the bases for the symbols that you selected.

Table 1.4. Public School Administrators Use Boilerplate

Groups	Response*	Explanation
Businesspeople—Prize For-Profit Schools		
Parents—Children in Public Schools		

*– Low
± Moderate
+ High

SUMMARY

Politicians came up with special strategies to deal with shrewd questions. They inspired educators to replicate their strategies.

2

WHAT IS INSTRUCTION'S GOAL?

Reading [education] is important.

—Timothy Shanahan, quoted by Rich, 2007

The main purpose of a Montessori school is to provide . . . creative learning.

—"Goals of a Montessori School," 2009

Pressure to produce high math and English test scores [has] made it tough . . . to squeeze in . . . arts.

—Lisa Fleisher, 2013

[KIPP charter schools] focused on helping students in underserved communities climb the mountain to . . . college.

—KIPP Foundation, 2013

Numerous groups were ready to identify the ultimate goal of instruction. However, they could not agree on it.

GOAL OF PROSPERITY

Social scientists investigated behavioral patterns. They then published their conclusions in scholarly journals. Although they attracted the attention of professional colleagues, they rarely enticed the general public. They asked journalists to assist them.

The journalists were willing to share the scholars' research with a large audience. However, they insisted that they highlight controversial conclusions. They gave them an example from the 1970s.

A group of scholars had studied prosperity and happiness. They noted that prosperity provided financial independence, political power, superior education, physical comfort, extensive leisure, rarefied medical care, and community respect. They assumed that it made individuals happy.

The scholars had devised an ingenious way to test the strength of the link between prosperity and happiness. They asked individuals who had won mammoth lottery prizes whether they became happier.

The scholars drew a counterintuitive conclusion: they judged that the lottery winners became less happy. They were excited when journalists publicized their results and members of the public applauded them (Brickman, Coates, & Janoff-Bulman, 1978; Dahl, 2012).

Scholars continued to examine the relationship between prosperity and happiness. In one examination, they posed two questions. They asked individuals whether they were happy; they also asked them how much money they earned annually.

The scholars concluded that individuals required seventy-five thousand dollars to be happy. Moreover, they judged that any additional money would not make them happier. They were excited when journalists publicized these counterintuitive conclusions and the public showed interest (Luscombe, 2010).

Some academicians were not persuaded by the research that challenged the link between wealth and happiness. They conducted their own studies, analyzed the results, and reaffirmed the conventional view of the two factors. Nonetheless, they were upset.

The academicians were upset when journalists ignored their research. The journalists predicted that members of the public would have little interest in it (Vanderkam, 2013).

GOAL OF EARLY INSTRUCTION

Even though the early teachers created curricula individually, they all placed a heavy emphasis on reading. They were aware of the value that their contemporaries placed on reading (Giordano, 2012b).

Teachers had ample evidence of reading's importance. They noticed that scholastic publishers had developed more textbooks for reading than any other academic subject. They also noted that educational researchers had made more investigations of reading than any other academic subject.

The teachers detected other evidence of reading's importance. They observed that entrepreneurs were establishing special, for-profit clinics to help students with reading problems. They also observed the many professors who were training specialists to help students with reading problems (Giordano, 2000, 2003, 2009).

Parents approved of the reading-centered curricula. Nonetheless, they worried that some teachers did not have the training that they needed to create sound curricula (Giordano, 2012b).

Scholastic publishers pledged to help the poorly trained teachers. They explained that they would commission expert-devised curricula and then place them within their textbooks (Giordano, 2003).

GOAL OF TWENTIETH-CENTURY INSTRUCTION

Most professors classified reading as the most important subject in the curriculum. Even though they pleased many of their contemporaries, they did not please everyone. They annoyed some of their colleagues.

The disgruntled professors were irked by literacy's academic cachet. They contended that special types of literacy, such as mathematical literacy, were just as important as verbal literacy (Klein, 2002; M. Kline, 1973; Pace, 1992).

The pro-mathematics professors realized that they would need allies if they were going to change the schools. They made appeals to the businesspeople who were involved in science, manufacturing, and engineering. They warned them that the currently inadequate mathematics instruction was threatening their ventures; they added that it eventually could threaten the nation's economy (Fiske, 1988).

The pro-mathematics professors asked military leaders to prioritize mathematical literacy. They reminded them that they needed mathematically literate persons to fill the many technical jobs in the armed services. They added that they also needed them to work in weapons laboratories. They warned that inadequate mathematics instruction could jeopardize these goals (Giordano, 2004, 2009, 2012b).

Businesspeople and military leaders agreed with the pro-mathematics professors. They placed pressure on teachers to expand and improve mathematics instruction. They continue to put pressure on them today (Anderson, 2007; Shea, 2012).

GOAL OF RECENT INSTRUCTION

After he won the presidential election of 1992, Bill Clinton vowed to concentrate on education. He promised to make it the hallmark of his administration.

Clinton pledged to improve academic instruction in the fundamental subjects: reading, mathematics, and the sciences. He added that he also would improve it in the foreign languages, the arts, and the social sciences.

Clinton conceded that his academic goals were ambitious. In fact, he claimed that they were too ambitious to be achieved quickly. He emphasized this point when he christened them the *Goals 2000*.

Advocating National Standards

Clinton embedded his academic goals into a congressional bill—*Goals 2000: Educate America Act*. He called for several educational reforms, including the adoption of national curricular standards (Goals 2000: Educate America Act, 1994).

Some persons were pleased when Clinton advocated national standards. Nonetheless, they realized that the standards could take years to develop. They looked for opportunities to expedite them (Walters, 1993; Starr, 1998).

The standards for mathematics were critically important. However, they did not need to be expedited; they already were available. A professional educational organization had formulated them several years before Clinton's bill was enacted (National Council of Teachers of Mathematics, 1989).

The standards for reading and writing, like those for mathematics, were critically important. Although they were not available at the time the legislation was enacted, they appeared soon afterward (IRA/NCTE Joint Task Force on Assessment, 1994).

Educators had anticipated national standards for reading, writing, and mathematics. They also anticipated them for the sciences (National Research Council, 1996).

Educators with expertise in reading, writing, mathematics, and the sciences were ebullient about the standards. They assumed that they would underscore the importance of their academic disciplines, improve the instruction in them, and lead to new resources.

Some educators were upset about support standards. They came from disciplines that did not have the same status as reading, writing, mathematics, and the sciences. They hoped to change their status. They lobbied federal politicians to designate standards for their disciplines.

The politicians acceded to the pressure from the lobbyists. They stated that they would specify standards for a wide range of disciplines: they sanctioned them for history, geography, foreign languages, the arts, physical education, and sports (Geography Education Standards Project, 1994; National Association for Sport and Physical Education, 2004; National Center for History in the Schools, 1996; National Standards in Foreign Language Education Project, 1999; Symposium on National Standards for Education in the Arts, 1994).

Criticizing National Standards

Clinton adjured teachers to support national standards. He stated that they should use them for classroom instruction and confirm their impact through standardized testing.

Not everyone supported Clinton. Some politicians opposed him because they believed that he was seizing educational authority from the states. However, they had additional reasons to oppose him on standards (Sunderman, 2009).

Some politicians judged that national standards would supersede their own educational aspirations. They aspired to make instruction more rigorous, standardized testing more pervasive, school choice more accessible, and teacher accountability more visible (Cheney, 1997; Ravitch, 1998).

Clinton rejoined that standards would achieve a wide range of goals. He stated that they had been designed in a way that would make instruction more demanding and standardized testing more common. He added that they would increase teacher accountability and expand school choice ("President Clinton: Announcing," 2000; Starr, 1998).

Clinton called for a bipartisan group of political supporters. He was pleased when this group grew large enough to enact the standards (Goals 2000: Educate America Act, 1994).

Some critics continued to oppose national standards after they had been authorized. Nonetheless, even the fiercest opponents were impressed by the political demeanor that Clinton had demonstrated. They advised his successor, George W. Bush, to assume the same demeanor.

Bush copied many of Clinton's educational policies: he pledged to expand first-rate instruction, standardized testing, teacher accountability, and school choice. He also pledged to enforce national educational standards (Giordano, 2011, 2012a, 2012b).

When Obama became president, he was given the same advice as his predecessors. He was directed to express a commitment to several key measures, including national standards.

Obama promised billions of dollars to the states that moved forward with national standards. By the end of his first term, he had convinced more than half of them to adopt them (Lewin, 2010).

Republican politicians were incensed when Obama embraced national standards. Even though they also had embraced them, they insisted that they had changed their minds (Burke & Marshall, 2010; Greene, 2012).

EXAMINING TELEOLOGICAL QUESTIONS

Groups were eager to designate an ultimate goal for scholastic instruction. However, they did not agree on it.

Activity 2.1

Scholars were asked about the connection of money to happiness. Some of them were skeptical: they detected a weak connection. How did groups respond?

Table 2.1 identifies two groups: journalists and members of the public.

Complete the table by indicating the ways in which groups responded to the skeptical scholars. You can use symbols.

Use the symbol – if groups expressed low confidence in them. Use the symbol ± for moderate confidence and the symbol + for high confidence. As a final step, explain the bases for the symbols that you selected.

You can rely on the information in this chapter, additional information, or the information cited in the references. If you are reading this chapter with colleagues, you can confer with them.

Table 2.1. Scholars Raise Questions about the Link between Money and Happiness

Groups	Response*	Explanation
Journalists		
Members of the Public		

*– Low
 ± Moderate
 + High

Activity 2.2

The early teachers were asked about the connection of reading to scholastic success. They detected a strong connection. How did groups respond?

Table 2.2 identifies four groups: parents, textbook publishers, the entrepreneurs who established for-profit reading clinics, and the professors who trained reading specialists.

Complete the table by indicating the ways in which the groups responded to the early teachers. You can use symbols.

Use the symbol – if groups expressed low confidence in them. Use the symbol ± for moderate confidence and the symbol + for high confidence. As a final step, explain the bases for the symbols that you selected.

Table 2.2. Early Teachers Detect a Link between Reading and Scholastic Success

Groups	Response*	Explanation
Parents		
Textbook Publishers		
Entrepreneurs—For-Profit Reading Clinics		
Professors—Train Reading Specialists		

*– Low
 ± Moderate
 + High

Activity 2.3

Professors were asked about the connection of mathematics to scholastic success. Some of them detected a strong connection. How did groups respond?

Table 2.3 identifies two groups: businesspeople and military leaders.

Complete the table by indicating the ways in which groups responded to the pro-mathematics professors. You can use symbols.

Use the symbol – if groups expressed low confidence in them. Use the symbol ± for moderate confidence and the symbol + for high confidence. As a final step, explain the bases for the symbols that you selected.

Table 2.3.   Professors Detect a Link between Mathematics and Scholastic Success

Groups	Response*	Explanation
Businesspeople		
Military Leaders		

*– Low
± Moderate
+ High

Activity 2.4

American presidents were asked about the connection of national standards to scholastic success. Some of them detected a strong connection. How did groups respond?

Table 2.4 identifies three groups: politicians aligned with President Clinton, those aligned with President George W. Bush, and those aligned with President Obama.

Complete the table by indicating the ways in which groups responded to the three pro-standards presidents. You can use symbols.

Use the symbol – if groups expressed low confidence in them. Use the symbol ± for moderate confidence and the symbol + for high confidence. As a final step, explain the bases for the symbols that you selected.

Table 2.4.   Presidents Detect a Link between National Standards and Scholastic Success

Groups	Response*	Explanation
Politicians—Aligned with Clinton		
Politicians—Aligned with George W. Bush		
Politicians—Aligned with Obama		

*– Low
 ± Moderate
 + High

SUMMARY

Numerous groups identified an ultimate goal for instruction. However, they did not identify the same goal.

3

WHAT ARE THE FUNDAMENTAL SUBJECTS?

The curriculum of the public school . . . includes . . . roller skating, Indian yells, wading, swimming, fire-making, fire-extinguishing, softball, hard ball, top-spinning, and . . . tree-climbing.

—F. H. Gabrielson & Edward Kahn, 1949

We, the leaders of American business and higher education, call on Congress to . . . improve student achievement in math and science.

—Business Roundtable, 2007

In Massachusetts, the likely result of the Common Core [Curriculum] is that the gains of the past 20 years will slowly but surely recede.

—Jamie Gass & Charles Chieppo, 2013

Persons asked speculative and factual questions about business. They made an impression on the persons who were posing questions about education.

INVESTMENT FUNDAMENTALS

Executives at publicly traded companies wished to attract investors. They asked marketing experts to help them.

The marketing experts were ready to assist. They highlighted the media campaigns that they had used to promote commercial products. They recommended similar campaigns to lure investors.

The executives were impressed by the media campaigns. Nonetheless, they realized that investors were not completely satisfied.

Investors wanted information about the financial prospects for companies. They also wanted to know about the prospects for the banking industry, the stock market, the national economy, and international markets. They referred to this as technical information.

After the investors had received technical information, they still were not satisfied. They asked about the financial histories of the companies in which they were interested. They referred to this as fundamental information.

Facebook

Businesspeople valued fundamental information. They were particularly interested in information about the prices for which stocks had traded.

Businesspeople became nervous when they did not have information about stock prices. Nonetheless, they realized that they sometimes could not obtain it. They could not obtain it when a privately held business was being transformed into a publicly traded company. They faced this problem with Facebook (Gregoriou, 2006; Zattoni & Judge, 2012).

Facebook had been established in 2004. It was privately managed for the next eight years.

Investors were excited when Facebook executives announced that they would orchestrate an initial public offering (IPO). They were impressed by the wealth that the other technology corporations had generated for investors during IPOs; they hoped that Facebook would present a comparable opportunity.

The executives at Facebook had to determine the amount that they would raise during the IPO. They referred to this amount as market capitalization. They could influence it by the number of shares that they offered and the price that they tried to set for them.

The executives were nervous that government regulators, independent financial experts, and media analysts would question their decisions about share prices. They noted that some groups already had designated twenty dollars as the fair price for a Facebook share. They asked financial advisors to ensure that the final asking price was lucrative but also defensible (Barlyn & Vlastelica, 2012).

The financial advisors were determined to set the Facebook share price higher than twenty dollars. They eventually set it at thirty-eight dollars.

Skeptics

The Facebook executives kept their eyes on the post-IPO price of their stock. They became nervous when it declined. They became alarmed when it declined by more than one-third.

Some of the executives were alarmed about their personal losses. Others were alarmed about investors' losses. They anticipated that the investors would accuse the executives of manipulating stock prices in order to take windfall profits (Ortutay, 2012).

Investors who lost money after the Facebook IPO stated the executives' actions had been unprofessional. In fact, some of them claimed that the actions had been illegal. They grew angrier after they learned about executives who selectively had shared information about the indefensibly high IPO share prices (Cowan, 2012a, 2012b; Raice, Das, & Chon, 2012).

Journalists and investors scolded the Facebook executives for compromising the financial future of their company. Some claimed that they had compromised the IPO prospects for all private technology companies (Thurm, Raice, & Demos, 2012).

ACADEMIC FUNDAMENTALS

When businesspeople posed technical questions, they expected speculative responses. When they posed fundamental questions, they expected factual responses. They made an impression on the individuals who were investigating education.

Early Academic Curricula

Early teachers were not supplied with curricula. They had to devise them on their own.

Some teachers relied on their early experiences. They replicated the curricula to which they had been exposed by their own teachers.

Some teachers relied on later experiences. They fashioned curricula from the academic and pedagogical information that they had acquired in college (Giordano, 2012b).

Some teachers relied on commercial textbooks. They consulted materials about reading, writing, grammar, spelling, penmanship, mathematics, geography, history, or literature; they then extracted de facto curricula from them (Giordano, 2003).

Teachers sometimes did not have textbooks for the specific subject on which they were focusing. They created that curriculum with books on a distinct subject. They discovered that textbooks about history contained troves of information about topics such as religion, government, art, rhetoric, ethics, and music (Giordano, 2003).

Alternative Reading Curricula   Early teachers stressed reading. They realized that parents, religious leaders, businesspeople, and politicians demanded this emphasis (Giordano, 2009).

Most teachers taught reading by requiring children to memorize letters, words, phrases, sentences, and passages. They assumed that those who could complete these tasks were literate.

Not all persons had confidence in memorization-based curricula. Critics questioned whether the students who recited passages actually comprehended them. They also questioned whether they could decipher words that they never had encountered.

The teachers who employed memorization-based literacy curricula were badgered relentlessly. Although they tried to make corrective adaptations to their current curricula, they were forced to adopt alternative curricula.

Some of the teachers adopted kinesthetic curricula. They required students to make physical movements corresponding to the meanings of words, phrases, or sentences. They claimed that these curricula were effective because of the peculiar way that they reinforced comprehension.

Some teachers used phonics curricula. They encouraged their students to enunciate the sounds of letters and then blend them into words. They claimed that their students then would be able to decipher unfamiliar words (Giordano, 2000).

Teachers experimented with technology-based curricula. They required students to read passages that were displayed with projectors or recited on phonograph records. They claimed that the students would be motivated by these curricula.

Teachers used children's literature curricula. They encouraged students to read high-interest books; they hoped that they would be more enticed by these materials than basal readers.

Teachers used oral-language curricula. They conversed with children, transcribed their conversations, and then encouraged them to read the transcriptions. They claimed that these curricula simplified learning to read (Giordano, 2000).

Common Curricula   Educational critics knew that the early teachers were creating their own literacy curricula. They doubted that they were qualified.

The critics wanted to be sure that teachers used curricula that gave children opportunities to master fundamental literacy skills. Convinced that few teachers could devise them on their own, they adjured them to implement common curricula. They explained that common curricula, which had been assembled by teams of expert educators, were detailed, comprehensive, and effective.

By the late 1800s, the teachers in large school districts were using common curricula for reading. They frequently were using them for other subjects as well.

Progressive Curricula

John Dewey emerged as a prominent scholastic critic during the late 1800s. He and like-minded critics identified themselves as progressive educators. They attracted attention through their challenges of prevalent instructional practices.

Dewey discouraged the heavy emphasis on reading. He explained that reading was an antiquated *fetish* that had little value for modern students (Giordano, 2000).

Dewey also discouraged teachers from employing common curricula. He was especially annoyed with those who also were employing uniform instructional strategies and universal learning materials.

Dewey adjured teachers to be sensitive to the eccentricities of individual children. In fact, he and the other progressive educators instructed them to allow children to design their own curricula (Giordano, 2000, 2009).

The progressive educators encouraged teachers to get involved with liberal political organizations; some urged them to join the Communist Party. They pressed them to share their political convictions with their students.

The progressive educators attracted thousands of adherents during the Great Depression. Nonetheless, they soon alienated most of them. They estranged both teachers and members of the public with their combination of extremely liberal political and scholastic advice.

Holistic Curricula

The progressive educators had almost vanished by the early 1950s. They emerged again a decade later.

The new progressive educators retained many of the earlier beliefs. They still prized politically liberal government initiatives. They still disparaged common curricula, uniform instructional strategies, and universal learning materials.

The new progressive educators changed their name: they stated that they were *whole-child educators*. They made another change that was more substantive: they stated that reading instruction was critically important.

Some persons were alarmed by the whole-child educators. They had questions about the ways that they provided instruction, designed curricula, selected learning materials, and assessed progress (Giordano, 2005, 2010).

Back-to-Basics Curricula

The whole-child educators hoped that their passion would give them an advantage during confrontations with critics. They soon realized that their critics also were passionate.

The critics identified reading, writing, and mathematics as fundamental academic subjects. They maintained that they constituted the foundation for the rest of the curriculum. They worried that the students who were learning with holistic curricula were not developing that foundation. They wanted to see assessment information about those students' progress.

The whole-child educators were ready to supply critics with information about students' progress in reading, writing, and mathematics. They explained that they would furnish their personal observations. They also promised to furnish portfolios of students' classwork.

The critics were not interested in observations and portfolios; they complained that they were too subjective. They demanded a different type of evidence: they wanted standardized academic achievement tests.

The whole-child teachers opposed standardized tests. They stated that these tests were not sensitive to the idiosyncrasies of schools, teachers, and students. They reminded the critics that they had rejected common curricula and uniform instructional strategies for similar reasons.

The critics were unimpressed by the rejoinders from the whole-child teachers. Moreover, they believed that these teachers were arrogant. They resolved to put greater pressure on them. They searched for allies.

The critics surprised the whole-child teachers with the allies that they attracted: they lured many parents and politicians. With the support of these powerful groups, they forced the teachers to use standardized tests for reading, writing, and mathematics (Fiske, 1988; Giordano, 2000; Maeroff, 1975, 1977).

The whole-child teachers were upset about the standardized tests. They predicted that the competencies in them would not align with those in their classrooms. They were correct.

The whole-child teachers predicted that the students in their classrooms would score poorly on standardized tests. Once again, they were correct.

Critics gloated when the students in holistic learning programs scored poorly on standardized tests. They advised the teachers to adopt new curricula. They recommended curricula that emphasized fundamental academic skills; they referred to them as *back-to-basics* curricula.

The back-to-basics enthusiasts wanted teachers to identify, emphasize, standardize, and assess essential academic skills. They concentrated on the skills in reading, writing, and mathematics (Carnoy, Elmore, & Siskin, 2003; McDermott, 2011).

Scholars in several disciplines were beguiled by the back-to-basics enthusiasts. They applied their philosophy to disparate fields, including business, the ministry, and the military (Banks, 2008; Demarest, 2011; McClurg & Brighty, 2004).

The back-to-basics enthusiasts elicited strong national support during the 1970s. However, they lost most of it by the end of that decade. They lost support after their curriculum did little to improve student achievement.

Even though they could not retain their national constituency, the back-to-basics enthusiasts remained vibrant in several states. They lured many supporters from Texas during the 1980s; they still lure significant numbers of supporters from that state today (Alpert, Gorth, & Allan, 1989; Conner, Chadwick-Joshua, Parks, Truscott, & Wajngurt, 2012).

STEM Curricula

The back-to-basics teachers were distressed when the public's approval of them declined. They resolved to transform themselves.

The repackaged back-to-basics enthusiasts continued to emphasize reading, writing, and mathematics. However, they made two important changes.

The new enthusiasts placed a stronger emphasis on mathematics. They also placed a stronger emphasis on the careers to which mathematics was linked: those in science, technology, and engineering.

The enthusiasts had an acronym for the type of curriculum that they endorsed: STEM. They explained that this term comprised the initial letters of four key academic subjects: science, technology, engineering, and mathematics (Johnson, 2011).

The STEM proponents pitched their curriculum to parents. They told them that it would get their children ready for challenging, prestigious, and remunerative jobs.

The STEM proponents pitched their curriculum to business-people. They promised them that it would increase the number of

Americans who were applying for critically important jobs in their industries (Bilton, 2012; Business Roundtable, 2007; Gordon, 2012).

Proponents asserted that the STEM curriculum would benefit the entire nation. They explained that it would reduce America's reliance on foreign-born scientists, technology experts, engineers, and mathematicians. They reasoned that this independence would strengthen national security (Drew, 2011; Giordano, 2004; Kurtzleben, 2012; "Science, Technology, Engineering and Mathematics [STEM] Workforce Division," 2012).

The STEM proponents developed specialized curricula for elementary school students. They wanted to help them form positive attitudes toward key subjects and the academic skills to master those subjects (Bilton, 2012; Hu, 2010; Murphy, 2011).

Proponents were eager to devise STEM curricula for high school students. However, they needed help from university faculty and employers. They asked the faculty to admit their students into some university courses; they asked the employers to admit them into vocational internships (Johnson, 2011; Ruiz, 2012; "STEM schools," 2012).

The STEM proponents needed help from still more groups. They asked state and federal politicians to endorse their curricula. They were excited when they overwhelmingly signaled approval ("California Business," 2012; Nagel, 2009; Ruiz, 2012).

The politicians did not hesitate to endorse the STEM curricula. Nonetheless, some of them initially were not ready to supply the funds to implement them ("STEM Grants," 2012; United States Committee on Science and Technology, 2007).

The politicians eventually did give the STEM enthusiasts substantial funding. However, they set conditions: the recipients of the funding needed to employ common instruction, curricula, assessment, and learning materials (Huffman & Lawrenz, 2006; United States National Research Council, 2011).

EXAMINING FUNDAMENTAL QUESTIONS

Businesspeople asked some questions to which they expected speculative answers; they asked others to which they expected factual answers. They made an impression on the persons with questions about education.

Activity 3.1

Facebook executives were asked questions during their firm's IPO. They could not answer questions about financial fundamentals. How did groups respond?

Table 3.1 identifies two groups: the investors with key information about overpriced IPO stock shares and the investors without that key information.

Complete the table by indicating the ways in which the groups responded to the Facebook executives. You can use symbols.

Use the symbol – if groups exhibited low confidence in them. Use the symbol ± for moderate confidence and the symbol + for high confidence. As a final step, explain the bases for the symbols that you selected.

You can rely on the information in this chapter, additional information, or the information cited in the references. If you are reading this chapter with colleagues, you can confer with them.

Table 3.1.   Facebook Executives Are Quizzed about Financial Fundamentals

Groups	Response*	Explanation
Investors with Key Information		
Investors without Key Information		

*– Low
 ± Moderate
 + High

Activity 3.2

The early teachers were asked for evidence that students were mastering reading fundamentals. They had difficulty supplying it. How did groups respond?

Table 3.2 identifies two groups: educational critics who espoused alternative reading curricula and those who espoused common curricula.

Complete the table by indicating the ways in which the groups responded to the early teachers. You can use symbols.

Use the symbol – if groups exhibited low confidence in them. Use the symbol ± for moderate confidence and the symbol + for high confidence. As a final step, explain the bases for the symbols that you selected.

Table 3.2. Early Teachers Are Quizzed about Reading Fundamentals

Groups	Response*	Explanation
Critics—Espouse Alternative Curricula		
Critics—Espouse Common Curricula		

*– Low
 ± Moderate
 + High

Activity 3.3

Progressive teachers were asked for evidence that students were mastering academic fundamentals. They had difficulty supplying it. How did groups respond?

Table 3.3 identifies four groups: teachers with liberal attitudes about pedagogy, teachers with conservative attitudes about pedagogy, members of the public with liberal attitudes about politics, and members of the public with conservative attitudes about politics.

Complete the table by indicating the ways in which the groups responded to the progressive teachers. You can use symbols.

Use the symbol – if groups exhibited low confidence in them. Use the symbol ± for moderate confidence and the symbol + for high confidence. As a final step, explain the bases for the symbols that you selected.

Table 3.3. Progressive Teachers Are Quizzed about Academic Fundamentals

Groups	Response*	Explanation
Teachers— Pedagogically Liberal		
Teachers— Pedagogically Conservative		
Members of the Public—Politically Liberal		
Members of the Public—Politically Conservative		

*– Low
 ± Moderate
 + High

Activity 3.4

Back-to-basics teachers were asked for evidence that students were mastering academic fundamentals. They readily supplied it. How did groups respond?

Table 3.4 identifies two groups: educational critics who placed a high priority on standardized tests and those who placed a high priority on reading, writing, and mathematics.

Complete the table by indicating the ways in which the groups responded to the back-to-basics teachers. You can use symbols.

Use the symbol – if groups exhibited low confidence in them. Use the symbol ± for moderate confidence and the symbol + for high confidence. As a final step, explain the bases for the symbols that you selected.

Table 3.4. Back-to-Basics Teachers Are Quizzed about Academic Fundamentals

Groups	Response*	Explanation
Critics—Prioritize Standardized Tests		
Critics—Prioritize Reading, Writing, and Mathematics		

*– Low
± Moderate
+ High

Activity 3.5

The STEM teachers were asked for evidence that students were mastering academic fundamentals. They readily supplied it. How did groups respond?

Table 3.5 identifies three groups: parents, businesspeople, and politicians.

Complete the table by indicating the ways in which the groups responded to the STEM teachers. You can use symbols.

Use the symbol – if groups exhibited low confidence in them. Use the symbol ± for moderate confidence and the symbol + for high confidence. As a final step, explain the bases for the symbols that you selected.

Table 3.5. STEM Teachers Are Quizzed about Academic Fundamentals

Groups	Response*	Explanation
Parents		
Businesspeople		
Politicians		

*– Low
± Moderate
+ High

SUMMARY

Businesspeople expected speculative answers to some questions; they expected factual answers to others. They made an impression on the persons who had questions about education.

4

WHAT PRODS LEARNING?

Pay to learn is working.

—Anne Stuhldreher, 2008

If you don't starve the [school] system, you won't make it change.

—Nick Pandelidis, quoted by Levitz, 2011

[School districts] have received federal money . . . to experiment with performance-based pay.

—Erin Richards, 2012

Unions . . . say that isolating the effect of a given teacher is harder than it seems.

—Annie Lowrey, 2012

Psychologists used incentives to change behaviors. They made an impression on teachers, who used them with students. They also made an impression on politicians, who used them with teachers.

DRIVERS

Groups were upset by the damages, injuries, and deaths that automobile drivers caused when they sped through red traffic lights. They wanted to change their behaviors.

Police

Police had a plan to affect the drivers: they would give them information about the terrible consequences of running lights. They noted that the plan would be easy to administer and fund. They were eager to experiment.

The officers were disappointed with the information campaign. They conceded that it failed to reduce reckless driving. They searched for another plan.

The officers traditionally had issued fines to the drivers who violated traffic regulations. They proposed to hide near the traffic lights, keep a lookout for bad drivers, and aggressively issue tickets.

The officers were sure that drivers viewed tickets as punishments. They predicted that they would change their behaviors to avoid them.

Although the officers had confidence in their plan, they acknowledged that they only could station a limited number of persons at traffic lights. They anticipated that they would have to divert officers from other assignments or hire additional personnel.

Entrepreneurs

Entrepreneurs had their own plan to reduce reckless driving. They wished to install cameras at traffic lights. They then would photograph violators, use official records to locate them, send tickets to them, and collect fines (Wells, 2012).

The entrepreneurs stated that their plan would require no funding. In fact, they promised that it would generate revenue.

The entrepreneurs explained that the money from fines would pay for equipment, staff, and operating costs. However, money still would be left over. They would give a portion of it to cash-strapped municipal officials and keep the rest as profit.

Community groups were excited by the entrepreneurs' plan. Some of them were excited because they wished to deter reckless drivers: they reasoned that these drivers would change their behaviors. Others were excited because they competed for public funds: they reasoned that the pool of funds would grow larger. They asked their local politicians to commission the cameras.

Many politicians were eager to install cameras. They assumed that they would promote safety; they were sure that they would generate revenue. They pledged to give some of the revenue to the police, whom they asked to endorse the plan.

Like the politicians, the police endorsed the red-light cameras. They calculated that they would generate millions of dollars for large cities (Johnson, 2009; Mack, 2012).

Skeptics

Some persons were not convinced that the red-light cameras were effective. They wanted data from the communities that had installed them. For example, they wanted data about side-of-car and rear-of-car accidents.

The skeptics discovered that side-of-car accidents did decrease after the installation of cameras. However, rear-of-car collisions increased. They reasoned that they increased because drivers were braking suddenly to avoid cameras ("Lights, Cameras, Reaction," 2013).

The skeptics requested still more information from communities with red-light cameras. They wanted to know about improvements in automobile safety, traffic management, road construction, and consumer technology. They attempted to determine the extent to which these improvements had contributed to the declining accident rates (Flegenheimer, 2012; Giordano, 2010).

Some skeptics were concerned that volunteer firefighters and emergency vehicle operators would be penalized unfairly. They noted that they could have legitimate reasons to make unorthodox vehicular maneuvers. Although these reasons could be explained to police officers, they could not be explained to inanimate cameras (Flegenheimer, 2012).

Some of the skeptics judged that the red-light cameras were unconstitutional. They contended that they compromised citizens' rights to privacy and due process (Johnson, 2009; Koppel, 2011).

Skeptics noted the entrepreneurs who spent hundreds of thousands of dollars lobbying for red-light cameras. They judged that they displayed complex conflicts of interests. They were furious when entrepreneurs persuaded politicians to reduce the length of the span during which traffic lights flashed yellow ("Lights, Cameras, Reaction," 2013).

STUDENTS

Teachers assumed that students' attitudes could enhance or undermine instruction. However, they were unable to link this assumption to a sound theory of learning. They turned to psychologists for help.

Psychologists

Psychologists had investigated the factors influencing animals' behaviors. They had looked carefully at incentives.

The psychologists were interested in positive incentives, such as food. They had wondered how animals would react when their food was regulated.

The psychologists observed that animals changed their behaviors to obtain food. They noted that they then maintained their new behaviors after their food was no longer manipulated (Mead, 1934; Skinner, 1974; Sobel, 1990; Watson, 1970).

The psychologists were interested in negative as well as positive incentives. They wondered how animals would react to punishments.

The psychologists were impressed when animals changed their behaviors to avoid punishments. They also were impressed when they then maintained their new behaviors after the punishments had ceased (Brush & Black, 1971; Campbell & Church, 1969; Reilly & Schachtman, 2009).

The psychologists claimed that their studies revealed extremely practical strategies. They added that they also revealed a powerful theory of learning.

The psychologists referred to their theory as *behaviorism*. They were sure that it was applicable to humans as well as animals.

Proponents detected opportunities to incorporate behaviorism into numerous disciplines: counseling, psychiatry, rehabilitation, criminal justice, military training, business management, and marketing. They detected especially rich opportunities in education.

Educators

Some teachers were interested in the behaviorists' strategies. Others were more interested in the theory of learning to which they were connected.

Teachers already had strategies to change students' behaviors. They had relied on personal intuitions and professional experiences to create them. For example, they had multiple strategies that they used to signal approval to students.

Some teachers signaled approval with gestures and comments. Others signaled it with small gifts, snacks, extra recess time, grades, diplomas, scholarships, and promotions (Kazdin, 1977; Scott, Anderson, & Alter, 2012).

Teachers continually searched for new ways to reward students. Some of them wished to pay them to learn. They looked for a group to underwrite the cost.

The teachers gave the businesspeople reasons to subsidize pay-to-learn programs. They assured them that they would prepare students to excel in classrooms. They added that they also would prepare them to excel later in competitive, incentive-driven workplaces (Boaler, 2008; Giordano, 2010).

Teachers used punishments along with rewards. Some of them punished students with censorious gestures, acerbic comments, lowered grades, delayed promotions, or withheld diplomas. Others used harsher punishments: they resorted to paddling, physical restraints, military-style drills, or isolation rooms.

Skeptics

Skeptics had concerns about teachers using punishments. They worried that they might lack the temperaments needed to employ them effectively (Donnelly & Straus, 2005).

Skeptics examined cases in which teachers had employed paddles, restraints, and isolation rooms. They noted that many of them had caused physical, social, or emotional injuries to students (Bialik, 2009; Bitensky, 2006; Lichtenstein, 2012; Saunders & Goddard, 2010).

Skeptics had doubts about teachers who linked behaviorist theory to punitive classroom strategies. They worried that they were focusing on simple behaviors but ignoring complex, creative, and maturational behaviors (Rosen, Carrier, & Cheever, 2010; Silver, Strong, & Perini, 2000).

Although skeptics raised questions about the teachers who employed stern punishments, they also raised them about the groups that endorsed them. They had multiple questions for the politicians who endorsed them.

Skeptics conceded that some politicians believed that punishments were in the best interests of students. However, they suspected that others viewed them as a cheap foundation for scholastic reform. They explained that the funding needed for punishments was much less than that needed for teachers, auxiliary staffs, facilities, technology, textbooks, an extension of the school year, reductions of class sizes, or in-service training (Giordano, 2010, 2012a).

TEACHERS

Critics were annoyed by ineffective schools; they were especially annoyed by the teachers in them. They judged that the teachers were not doing enough for their students.

School Critics

The critics identified ways for teachers to help students. They recommended that they embrace standardized tests, report their students' scores on the tests, and personally accept the responsibility for those scores.

The critics were sure that their recommendations would raise test scores. They were sure that they also would make the teachers more accountable to the public.

The critics explained that connecting individual teachers to their students' test scores would indicate how hard those teachers were working. They had a way to motivate those who were not working hard: they would use the test scores to determine their salaries (Giordano, 2012a; Strauss, 2010).

The teachers protested that students' test scores could not be used to determine raises. They stated that the scores were influenced by factors that teachers did not control.

The critics were upset that teachers resisted salary incentives. They considered their arguments to be specious. They noted that the teachers already had supported incentives for students (Giordano, 2012a, 2012b; "School Reform on the Ballot," 2012).

The teachers wished to tie raises to schedules. They explained that the schedules provided raises after they completed specified periods of service (Giordano, 2012a).

The critics opposed the salary schedules. They complained that they gave dollars to ineffective as well as effective teachers. They preferred to lavish dollars exclusively on the effective teachers. They predicted that their plan would sustain the behaviors of the effective teachers and alter those of the others.

The critics were startled by the force with which the skeptics resisted salary incentives. They realized that they needed forceful allies. During the administration of George W. Bush, they persuaded the president and key persons within his administration to serve as their political champions (Turner, 2010).

Skeptics

Teachers realized that the school critics were extremely ardent. They were able to assemble advocates who were just as ardent.

The teachers' advocates were skeptical of salary incentives. They contended that superior instruction was too complex to be coupled to students' scores. They predicted that this coupling would dispirit competent teachers and confuse struggling teachers (Peterson, 2006; Vairo, Marcus, & Weiner, 2007).

The skeptics had another reason for objecting to salary incentives: they stated that they would have little effect on students' test scores. They identified multiple cases in which these incentives had failed to affect those scores (Strauss, 2010; Toppo, 2010; Wragg, 2004).

The skeptics needed their own political champion. They had difficulty attracting one during the Bush administration. They expected to be more successful after a successor took office. Having robustly contributed to Barack Obama's presidential campaign, they expected him to take their side on test-based raises.

Obama surprised the skeptics: he announced that he supported salary incentives. He stated that he would earmark hundreds of millions of dollars for the schools that implemented them (Richards, 2012; United States Department of Education, 2012).

EXAMINING PSYCHOLOGICAL QUESTIONS

Psychologists used incentives to alter behaviors. They made an impression on teachers, who applied incentives to students. They also made an impression on politicians, who applied them to teachers.

Activity 4.1

Entrepreneurs contended that reckless drivers were affected by red-light cameras. How did groups respond?

Table 4.1 identifies three groups: cash-strapped municipal officials, community groups, and reckless drivers.

Complete the table by indicating how the groups responded to the entrepreneurs. You can use symbols.

Use the symbol – if groups demonstrated low confidence in them. Use the symbol ± for moderate confidence and the symbol + for high confidence. As a final step, explain the bases for the symbols that you selected.

You can rely on the information in this chapter, additional information, or the information cited in the references. If you are reading this chapter with colleagues, you can confer with them.

Activity 4.2

Politicians contended that reckless drivers were affected by red-light cameras. How did groups respond?

Table 4.1.   Entrepreneurs Contend that Red-Light Cameras Affect Driver Behaviors

Groups	Response*	Explanation
Municipal Officials		
Community Groups		
Reckless Drivers		

*– Low
± Moderate
+ High

Table 4.2.   Politicians Contend that Red-Light Cameras Affect Driver Behaviors

Groups	Response*	Explanation
Police Officers		
Volunteer Firefighters		
Individuals—Worry about Constitutional Rights		

*– Low
± Moderate
+ High

Table 4.2 identifies three groups: police officers, volunteer firefighters, and individuals who worried especially about infringements on constitutional rights.

Complete the table by indicating how the groups responded to the politicians. You can use symbols.

Use the symbol – if groups demonstrated low confidence in them. Use the symbol ± for moderate confidence and the symbol + for high confidence. As a final step, explain the bases for the symbols that you selected.

Activity 4.3

Psychologists contended that students were motivated by rewards. How did groups respond?

Table 4.3 identifies two groups: teachers who espoused modest rewards for students and businesspeople who subsidized pay-to-learn programs in the schools.

Complete the table by indicating how the groups responded to the psychologists. You can use symbols.

Use the symbol – if groups demonstrated low confidence in them. Use the symbol ± for moderate confidence and the symbol + for high confidence. As a final step, explain the bases for the symbols that you selected.

Activity 4.4

Psychologists contended that students were motivated by punishments. How did groups respond?

Table 4.4 identifies two groups: teachers who espoused stern punishments for students and politicians who espoused them.

Complete the table by indicating how the groups responded to the psychologists. You can use symbols.

Use the symbol – if groups demonstrated low confidence in them. Use the symbol ± for moderate confidence and the symbol + for high confidence. As a final step, explain the bases for the symbols that you selected.

Table 4.3. Psychologists Contend that Rewards Affect Student Behaviors

Groups	Response*	Explanation
Teachers—Espouse Modest Rewards		
Businesspeople— Fund Pay-to-Learn		

*− Low
 ± Moderate
 + High

Table 4.4. Psychologists Contend that Punishments Affect Student Behaviors

Groups	Response*	Explanation
Teachers—Espouse Stern Punishments		
Politicians—Espouse Stern Punishments		

*− Low
 ± Moderate
 + High

Activity 4.5

Educational critics contended that public school teachers were motivated by test-based raises. How did groups respond?

Table 4.5 identifies two groups: politicians aligned with George W. Bush and those aligned with Barack Obama.

Complete the table by indicating how the groups responded to the educational critics. You can use symbols.

Use the symbol – if groups demonstrated low confidence in them. Use the symbol ± for moderate confidence and the symbol + for high confidence. As a final step, explain the bases for the symbols that you selected.

Table 4.5.   School Critics Contend that Test-Based Raises Affect Teacher Behaviors

Groups	Response*	Explanation
Politicians—Aligned with George W. Bush		
Politicians—Aligned with Barack Obama		

*– Low
 ± Moderate
 + High

Activity 4.6

Advocates of the public schools contended that the teachers were motivated by salary schedules. How did groups respond?

Table 4.6 identifies two groups: politicians aligned with George W. Bush and those aligned with Barack Obama.

Complete the table by indicating how the groups responded to the public school advocates. You can use symbols.

Use the symbol – if groups demonstrated low confidence in them. Use the symbol ± for moderate confidence and the symbol + for high confidence. As a final step, explain the bases for the symbols that you selected.

Table 4.6. School Advocates Contend that Salary Schedules Affect Teacher Behaviors

Groups	Response*	Explanation
Politicians—Aligned with George W. Bush		
Politicians—Aligned with Barack Obama		

*– Low
± Moderate
+ High

SUMMARY

Teachers and politicians were impressed by incentives. The teachers used them to stimulate students; the politicians used them to stimulate teachers.

5

HOW COMPLEX IS
CLASSROOM DISCIPLINE?

The chief complaint against public schools is that students do not receive enough discipline.

—Myron Farber, 1969

Supporters look at public military schools [as] . . . islands of stability in chaotic urban seas.

—Alina Tugend, 2005

Out-of-school suspensions have become the default punishment . . . for . . . displays of affection, dress-code violations, truancy, tardiness, [and] refusal to follow directions.

—Sarah Carr, 2012

[The] school board has voted to reinstate paddling.

—John O'Connor, 2013

[The student] was suspended from school . . . after arguing with a math teacher who had asked him to change seats.

—Erica Phillips, 2013

Some groups recommended that school discipline be strict; others recommended that it be lenient. They acknowledged that both approaches had complex consequences.

LEGAL QUESTIONS

Rick Perry was a long-serving governor in Texas. He aspired to a higher office: he wished to lead the nation.

Perry anticipated that some persons would question whether his experience as governor had prepared him to be president. He therefore highlighted key accomplishments.

Benefits of Tort Reform

Perry called attention to the state changes for which he was responsible. He called special attention to the new tort laws.

Individuals who had sustained personal injuries initiated tort suits. They attracted publicity when they won mammoth monetary awards. The awards and the procedures for assigning them were regulated by the civil laws in each state (Ruschmann, 2006).

Journalists conceded that Perry had been governor when the Texas tort laws were approved. However, they pointed out that legislators actually had enacted them. They asked him why he was taking credit for them.

Perry affirmed that the legislators had written the tort laws. Nonetheless, he insisted that they would not have enacted them without his vision and leadership.

Journalists had an additional concern about tort reform. They noted that the other presidential candidates had not discussed it. They asked Perry why he had taken a different tack.

Perry retorted that the other candidates had failed to appreciate the complex benefits of tort reform. He eagerly identified the benefits for Texas.

Perry contended that businesspeople were moving to Texas precisely because of its new tort laws. He explained that they realized they had relatively low chances of being convicted if Texas consumers brought legal actions against them ("Debunking the Myths," 2012; Sylvester, 2010).

Perry stated that the Texas courts had been able to operate more efficiently under the new tort laws. He explained that they had fewer cases because plaintiffs had slim chances of winning suits.

Perry claimed that the new laws had advanced justice in the Texas courts. He explained that they had made it difficult for clever lawyers to evoke inappropriately large payments from corporate defendants (Ruschmann, 2006).

Perry insisted that the new tort laws had helped businesspeople, corporations, and court officials. He was sure that they also had helped two other groups: physicians and patients.

Tort Reform and Healthcare

Journalists were not surprised when Perry stated that tort reform benefited physicians. However, they were surprised that he made the same claim about patients. After all, tort reform had made it more difficult for patients to sue physicians. They asked him to explain his reasoning.

Perry conceded that patients currently found it difficult to sue physicians in Texas. Nonetheless, he insisted that they benefited from reduced fees. He explained that physicians lowered their fees after their malpractice insurance became less expensive (Howard, 2009).

Perry identified another way that tort reform had helped patients: he alleged that it had expanded their access to medical providers. He explained that physicians no longer had to exit the state in order to purchase reasonably priced malpractice insurance (Smith, 2010).

Perry judged that tort reform had made medical services more affordable and available in Texas. He recommended it for other states (Krauthammer, 2009; Smith, 2010).

Skeptics

Not all healthcare analysts agreed with Perry. The skeptics concluded that he had disappointed patients because tort reform did not reduce their healthcare rates (Eviatar, 2009).

The skeptics judged that Perry had disappointed patients for still another reason. They explained that he had suppressed their opportunities to seek punitive awards from unprofessional physicians (Baker, 2005).

Some of the skeptics accused Perry of making tort reform into a political tool. They alleged that he had used it to reward the many physicians who had contributed to his campaign. They added that he had used it to penalize lawyers, who had contributed primarily to his opponent's campaign ("In Rambling Attack," 2012; Johnson, 2003; M. Smith, 2012).

Skeptics judged that Perry had conflicts of interests when he initially endorsed tort reform. They judged that he continued to have conflicts of interest when he later linked total reform to healthcare (Gawande, 2009).

EDUCATIONAL QUESTIONS

Parents wanted their children to behave in ways that helped them progress in schools. They hoped that they also would behave in ways that later would help them progress in workplaces.

Parents were perturbed when children did not behave. Needless to say, they were upset when they were delinquent or criminal. However, some were upset when they misbehaved mildly.

Discipline and Behavior

School critics were concerned about misbehaving youths. They noted the problems that the youths created for schools.

Although the critics worried about misbehaving youths during all eras, they became especially worried about them during times of war. They claimed that they created problems while they were in school and then later when they were members of the armed services.

Critics blamed several groups when youths misbehaved. They focused on teachers. They alleged that some of them were minimizing or ignoring classroom discipline.

The critics came up with strategies to help teachers reestablish discipline. They hoped that strategies with soldierly characteristics would draw the support of the nation's military leaders (Giordano, 2004).

The critics recommended marching drills. They noted that they easily could be incorporated into physical education courses. They predicted that they would have immediate benefits in classrooms and long-term benefits in military units.

Some school critics were not satisfied with marching activities. They encouraged teachers to introduce hand-to-hand combat, bayonet practice, and marksmanship.

The critics recommended strategies to draw the support of coaches. They stated that football would foster discipline. They explained that it developed the self-control, strength, coordination, and teamwork that the youths would require someday on battlefields (Giordano, 2004; Lee, 1983).

The critics also recommended nonphysical strategies to foster discipline. For example, they encouraged teachers to increase the academic rigor of instruction.

The critics were convinced that certain types of instruction, such as mathematics and science, were more rigorous than others. They contended that these subjects not only honed discipline but additional skills that were crucial to modern armies. They hoped that their endorsements of these subjects would elicit the support of the teachers who taught them.

The critics tried to elicit the support of employers. They told them that they recommended vocational instruction for those students who were struggling in precollegiate courses. They were sure that this instruction would prepare students for the home-front jobs that were essential to the nation's security.

The critics recommended that the students participate in paid vocational internships. They explained that they would develop discipline as they completed high school courses and labored at their jobs. They added that they also would fill the many home-front jobs that became vacant during wartime (Giordano, 2004).

School critics historically had praised classroom discipline as the way to reinvigorate schools. They continue to extol it for this reason today. They also continue to recommend strategies to foster it.

Critics still recommend competitive sports. However, they became more cautious after they were chastised for failing to highlight the physical dangers associated with these sports (Gerdy, 2000; Miracle & Rees, 1994; Pennington, 2013).

Critics continue to recommend military-style training. However, they became more cautious after they were accused of overstating the advantages and concealing the liabilities (Anderson, 2005; Trousdale, 2006).

Critics continue to recommend academically rigorous instruction. Nonetheless, they became more cautious after they were faulted for failing to validate the relationship of this instruction to discipline (Giordano; 2012b).

Discipline and Character

School critics adjured public school teachers to use stern discipline. They frequently encouraged them to model the disciplinary practices employed by the teachers in Catholic parochial schools (Walch, 1996).

The critics realized that the disciplinary practices in Catholic schools were connected to religious values. Although they did not expect public school teachers to adopt those values, they still encouraged them to implement the practices (Grace, 2002; Hunt, Joseph, & Nuzzi, 2001; Youniss, Convey, & McLellan, 2000).

Some persons maintained that corporal punishment was more prevalent in Catholic schools than in public schools. They were convinced that this punishment fostered important classroom character traits, such as cooperation, respect, and punctuality. They added that it fostered important out-of-classroom character traits, such as ethical conduct, moral awareness, and a sense of fairness (Turner, 2002).

Public school teachers in numerous countries had confidence in corporal punishment. Nonetheless, they had to abandon it after it was prohibited by national laws ("Boarding School Discipline," 1873; Giordano, 2009; Gould, 2007).

The teachers in America's early public schools did not have to worry about legal restrictions on corporal punishment. Although some of them are limited by state laws today, those in more than twenty states are unhindered (Donnelly & Straus, 2005; Randall, 2012).

The teachers who did not use stern disciplinary measures were taunted for failing to develop character. Although they may have been stung by this accusation, they refused to employ stern measures. They especially renounced corporal punishment, which they feared could cause physical and emotional damage.

The teachers who avoided corporal punishment did not disregard character. Many of them tried to develop it through gentle strategies: they arranged simulations, dramatizations, discussions of books, viewing of films, and role-playing with video games (Damon, 2002; Ellis, Morgan, & Reid, 2013; Lapsley & Power, 2005; Noddings, 2002; Nucci & Narváez, 2008).

Discipline and Academics

School critics were upset with teachers who did not discipline their students. They warned that they were undermining their conduct and character; they added that they were undermining their academic learning. They urged them to monitor and control their students strictly (Bear, 2010; Curwin, Mendler, & Mendler, 2008; Giordano, 2012b).

Many teachers did worry about misbehaving students. They acknowledged that they affected their own learning and that of their well-behaved peers. They resolved to supplement instruction with special disciplinary techniques; they referred to these techniques as *classroom management strategies* (Cummings, 2000; Evertson & Weinstein, 2006).

Proponents stated that classroom management strategies had two effects: they reduced classroom disruption and increased student learning. They provided examples of these strategies for every type of setting, from preschool through high school (Adams & Baronberg, 2005; Emmer, Evertson, Worsham, & Emmer, 2006).

Some persons questioned whether the classroom management strategies were really effective. They discovered cases in which they had failed to reduce bullying, drug distribution, weapons use, attacks on peers, and assaults on teachers. They recommended a stricter strategy—expulsion of disruptive students.

Proponents of expulsion acknowledged that teachers, principals, and school boards already were expelling students who committed extraordinary infractions. They urged them to also expel those who committed moderate or even routine infractions. They had a stark term for this strategy: *zero tolerance*.

Proponents of zero tolerance were criticized because this intervention did not address the causes of misbehavior. Although they conceded that this criticism was accurate, they insisted that their intervention still reduced misbehavior.

Proponents realized that zero tolerance was too controversial to be implemented without the support of influential allies. They requested aid from diverse groups: politicians, community leaders, school administrators, and parents. They were pleased when individuals from all these groups joined them (Kafka, 2011).

Opponents were not intimidated by the supporters of zero tolerance. They attempted to undermine them by demonstrating that they had conflicts of interest (Ayers, Dohrn, & Ayers, 2001).

The opponents identified other reasons why they did not have confidence in zero tolerance. They were perturbed about the way that it affected students. They complained that it expelled them even when exculpatory conditions were evident. They also noted that it disproportionately penalized students from minority groups (Lyons & Drew, 2006; Reyes, 2006; Western, 2006).

The opponents even were upset about the way that zero tolerance affected teachers. They contended that it prevented them from employing discretion. They reasoned that it hampered teachers in the same way that mandatory criminal sentencing hampered judges (Tierney, 2012).

EXAMINING COMPOUND QUESTIONS

Some groups detected problems in the courts; others detected them in the schools. Both groups recommended solutions with compound effects.

Activity 5.1

Texas Governor Perry contended that lenient tort laws benefited business. How did groups respond?

Table 5.1 identifies two groups: businesspeople and consumers in Texas.

Complete the table by indicating the ways in which groups responded to the Texas governor. You can use symbols.

Use the symbol – if groups demonstrated low confidence in him. Use the symbol ± for moderate confidence and the symbol + for high confidence. As a final step, explain the bases for the symbols that you selected.

Table 5.1. The Texas Governor Contends that Lenient Tort Laws Benefit Business

Groups	Response*	Explanation
Businesspeople		
Consumers		

*– Low
± Moderate
+ High

You can rely on the information in this chapter, additional information, or the information cited in the references. If you are reading this chapter with colleagues, you can confer with them.

Activity 5.2

Texas Governor Perry contended that lenient tort laws benefited the courts. How did groups respond?

Table 5.2 identifies two groups: plaintiffs who initiated industrial tort suits in Texas and the defendants in those cases.

Complete the table by indicating the ways in which groups responded to the Texas governor. You can use symbols.

Use the symbol – if groups demonstrated low confidence in him. Use the symbol ± for moderate confidence and the symbol + for high confidence. As a final step, explain the bases for the symbols that you selected.

Table 5.2.   The Texas Governor Contends that Lenient Tort Laws Improve Courts

Groups	Response*	Explanation
Plaintiffs		
Defendants		

*– Low
 ± Moderate
 + High

Activity 5.3

Texas Governor Perry contended that lenient tort laws benefited health-care. How did groups respond?

Table 5.3 identifies three groups: physicians, patients, and the lawyers who represented patients in malpractice suits.

Complete the table by indicating the ways in which groups responded to the Texas governor. You can use symbols.

Use the symbol – if groups demonstrated low confidence in him. Use the symbol ± for moderate confidence and the symbol + for high confidence. As a final step, explain the bases for the symbols that you selected.

Table 5.3. The Texas Governor Contends that Lenient Tort Laws Improve Healthcare

Groups	Response*	Explanation
Physicians		
Patients		
Lawyers		

*– Low
 ± Moderate
 + High

Activity 5.4

Proponents of strict classroom discipline contended that it improved students' conduct. How did groups respond?

Table 5.4 identifies five groups: parents, military leaders, business-people, mathematics/science teachers, and the school coaches for competitive team sports.

Complete the table by indicating the ways in which groups responded to proponents of strict classroom discipline. You can use symbols.

Use the symbol – if groups demonstrated low confidence in them. Use the symbol ± for moderate confidence and the symbol + for high confidence. As a final step, explain the bases for the symbols that you selected.

Table 5.4.   Proponents of Strict Classroom Discipline Contend that It Improves Conduct

Groups	Response*	Explanation
Parents		
Military Leaders		
Businesspeople		
Teachers—Mathematics & Science		
Coaches		

*– Low
 ± Moderate
 + High

Activity 5.5

Proponents of strict classroom discipline contended that it developed students' character. How did groups respond?

Table 5.5 identifies two groups: teachers who espoused corporal punishment and those who recommended gentler alternatives to it.

Complete the table by indicating the ways in which groups responded to proponents of strict classroom discipline. You can use symbols.

Use the symbol – if groups demonstrated low confidence in them. Use the symbol ± for moderate confidence and the symbol + for high confidence. As a final step, explain the bases for the symbols that you selected.

Table 5.5. Proponents of Strict Classroom Discipline Contend that It Develops Character

Groups	Response*	Explanation
Teachers—Espouse Corporal Punishment		
Teachers—Espouse Gentle Alternatives		

*– Low
  ± Moderate
  + High

Activity 5.6

Proponents of strict classroom discipline contended that it raised students' academic achievement. How did groups respond?

Table 5.6 identifies two groups: teachers who espoused classroom management strategies and those who espoused zero tolerance strategies.

Complete the table by indicating the ways in which groups responded to proponents of strict classroom discipline. You can use symbols.

Use the symbol – if groups demonstrated low confidence in them. Use the symbol ± for moderate confidence and the symbol + for high confidence. As a final step, explain the bases for the symbols that you selected.

Table 5.6. Proponents of Strict Classroom Discipline Contend that It Raises Academic Achievement

Groups	Response*	Explanation
Teachers—Espouse Classroom Management Strategies		
Teachers—Espouse Zero Tolerance Strategies		

*– Low
 ± Moderate
 + High

SUMMARY

Groups came up with multiple solutions to disciplinary problems. They acknowledged that all of them had compound results.

6

WHAT ARE THE RIGHT QUESTIONS ABOUT TEXTBOOKS?

That horrible mass of books . . . keeps on growing.

—Gottfried Leibniz, circa 1700, quoted by Gleick, 2011

If there was anything the human race had a sufficiency of, a sufficiency and a surfeit, it was books.

—Joseph Mitchell, 1996

Running a bookstore is a combat sport.

—Ministry of French Culture, quoted by Sciolino, 2012

E-books are either the savior or . . . the demise of book publishers.

—Charles Elder, quoted by Chen & Bosman, 2013

Industrialists posed some questions in order to bolster investors' confidence; they posed others to solve practical problems. They made an impression on scholastic publishers.

INDUSTRIALISTS

The Kodak Corporation had an impressive heritage: it had dominated the photographic industry for decades. However, it developed a distinct reputation after it lost market share, revenue, and profits (Spector & Mattioli, 2012).

Kodak executives were aware of their firm's decline. They began to pose strategic questions about the reasons for it. They hoped that those questions would reassure investors, solve practical problems, and restore industrial prominence.

Reassuring Investors

Kodak's executives used strategic questions to reassure investors. They focused these queries on their workers, managers, lawyers, and urban environment.

The executives asked whether the corporation's problems resulted from negotiations with organized labor. They then answered this question: they stated that former executives had made extremely imprudent concessions to the employees (Bussey, 2012a).

The executives asked whether their problems resulted from the size of their labor force. They blamed the former executives for hiring too many employees and an army of permanent, middle-level managers to supervise them (Mattioli & Fitzgerald, 2012).

The executives asked whether their problems were linked to Rochester, the city in which their corporation had centralized its physical facilities. They concluded that the city's numerous inadequacies had damaged the firm (Karlgaard, 2012).

The executives asked whether their problems should be attributed to lawyers. They answered that lawyers had damaged the company by delaying a series of key infringement-on-patent suits (Jones, 2012; Mattioli, Spector, & Jones, 2012; Spector, Mattioli, & Brickley, 2012).

Solving Practical Problems

Although Kodak's executives wished to reassure investors, they also wished to solve practical problems. They asked what could be done with current facilities, equipment, personnel, and patents.

The executives were particularly interested in Kodak's patents, which encompassed digital and film-based photographic technologies. They asked if the patents for the digital technologies were worth more than those for the film-based technologies.

Journalists and business analysts judged that the executives finally were asking the right questions. They noted that the answers to them could reassure the corporation's investors, restore its industrial stature, and solve the problems that had placed it in financial peril.

Even though they had praised the executives, the journalists and analysts still were disappointed with them. They explained that the executives had waited too long to ask the questions (Bussey, 2012b).

TEXTBOOK PUBLISHERS

Publishers realized that the textbook market had expanded for centuries. They expected it to keep growing.

The publishers were disconcerted when their market slowed down. They were shocked when it declined for several consecutive years (Barnes & Chozick, 2012; Trachtenberg, 2012).

Reassuring Consumers

Publishers looked for the cause of the weak market. They wondered whether consumers had changed their views of textbooks. They were particularly concerned about teachers, who influenced the learning materials that schools, districts, and states purchased.

The publishers asked teachers about textbooks. They listened attentively to their answers. They assured them that they would comply with any suggestions that they made.

Publishers took additional steps to ensure that they were responding to the advice of teachers. Some of them invited the teachers to serve as textbook critics; others hired them as authors. They hoped that this collaboration would raise quality and stimulate sales.

Publishers also queried parents about textbooks. They beamed when the parents stated that textbooks were an important way of compensating for weak teachers (Giordano, 2003, 2012a).

Publishers showcased testimonials from teachers and parents in marketing materials. They complemented them with endorsements from enthusiastic principals, superintendents, and school boards.

Solving Practical Problems

The textbook publishers wanted to determine the reason that their revenue was declining. They asked if consumers were losing confidence in their materials.

The publishers answered their own question. They asserted that consumers had revealed their confidence through the positive remarks that they had made about textbooks within surveys, interviews, and discussion groups.

Although the publishers were able to extract positive testimonials from many consumers, they conceded that some teachers were disgruntled. The disgruntled teachers complained frequently about the high prices of textbooks. Many principals, superintendents, school board members, and parents had the same complaint (Giordano, 2012a; Rado, 2010; Van Orsdel & Born, 2009).

Some publishers concluded that declining revenue should be attributed to prices. Others wished to ascribe it to a distinct factor: the competition from digital learning materials (Jacobs, 2011).

E-TEXTBOOK PUBLISHERS

When digital classroom materials emerged, textbook publishers were excited by the opportunities that they presented. They detected opportunities to cut production expenses for paper, printing, binding, warehousing, packaging, and shipping.

Although publishers realized that digital books would reduce their costs, they were not sure that they would increase their profits. They noted that the digital versions of trade books were priced at steep discounts; they predicted that the digital versions of textbooks would be priced at similar discounts (Engleman, 2009; Trachtenberg, 2011).

The publishers had another reason to question the profitability of e-textbooks: they worried about their amazing durability. Just as library personnel never had to replace worn-out e-books, school personnel would not have to replace worn-out e-textbooks (Stross, 2011).

The publishers worried about new retail competitors. They noted that Amazon, Apple, and other powerful retailers already had taken control of the digital trade book market. They feared that they would assume control of the digital textbook market as well (Bosman & Peters, 2011; Tibken, 2012).

Reassuring Consumers

The publishers were interested in ways that students viewed e-textbooks: they hoped that they considered them to be essential learning resources. Nonetheless, they knew that students had a limited impact on school purchases.

The publishers were primarily interested in teachers. They knew that they had a significant impact on school purchases. They hoped that they viewed e-textbooks as essential instructional tools.

Publishers attempted to identify the issues that were important to teachers. They realized that the prices were important to them. Even though e-textbook prices were lower than those for paper editions, they were compounded by the need to purchase electronic devices (Greenfield, 2012; Giordano, 2012a; Goleman & Norris, 2010).

The publishers assured teachers that they would be able to afford the devices on which to read e-textbooks. They stated that they could rely on relatively inexpensive equipment such as laptop computers, tablets, or even smartphones ("As E-book Market Evolves," 2013; Giordano, 2012a).

The publishers realized that the distinctive features of e-textbooks were important to teachers. They highlighted features such as animated illustrations, interactive tables, supplementary videos, learning games, and links to websites ("Scholastic Launches," 2013).

Publishers recognized that the attitudes of extra-scholastic groups were important to teachers when they gave advice about school materials. They asked parents, employers, and politicians how they felt about e-textbooks (Catalanello, 2010; "Device That Changed Everything," 2012; Hu, 2011).

The publishers answered their own question: they contended that the extra-scholastic groups valued e-textbooks. They explained that they valued them because they familiarized students with the latest technology.

They added that they also valued them because they speedily could accommodate curricular changes (Giordano, 2012a; Hoffman, 2011).

Solving Practical Problems

Publishers were concerned about the many school administrators and teachers who still were not ready to endorse e-textbooks. They asked why they were delaying.

The cautious school administrators were not sure that they could afford e-textbooks. They explained that they had not found a way to pay for the books, the portable electronic devices on which to read them, and the staffs to maintain the devices.

The cautious teachers acknowledged that students could use smartphones to display e-textbooks. However, they worried that they would have difficulty reading the small screens. They also worried about the many students who did not have smartphones (Giordano, 2012a).

The cautious teachers predicted that desktop computers would become the sole devices on which some students would read e-textbooks. Although they acknowledged that these computers had large monitors with sharp displays, they judged that they were much less practical than portable devices. In fact, they judged that they were much less practical than traditional paper textbooks.

POSING THE RIGHT QUESTIONS

Industrialists posed some questions to allay investor anxiety; they posed others to solve practical problems. They made an impression on scholastic publishers.

Activity 6.1

Executives at Kodak designed questions specifically to allay investor anxiety. How did groups respond?

Table 6.1 identifies four groups: the employees at Kodak, the middle-level managers at Kodak, the city officials in Rochester, and the lawyers at Kodak.

Complete the table by indicating the ways in which groups responded to the Kodak executives. You can use symbols.

Use the symbol – if groups exhibited low confidence in them. Use the symbol ± for moderate confidence and the symbol + for high confidence. As a final step, explain the bases for the symbols that you selected.

You can rely on the information in this chapter, additional information, or the information cited in the references. If you are reading this chapter with colleagues, you can confer with them.

Table 6.1. Executives Pose Questions to Allay Investor Anxiety about Kodak

Groups	Response*	Explanation
Employees		
Managers—Middle-Level		
City Officials—Rochester		
Lawyers		

*– Low
 ± Moderate
 + High

Activity 6.2

Executives at Kodak designed questions specifically to solve practical problems. How did groups respond?

Table 6.2 identifies two groups: journalists and business analysts.

Complete the table by indicating the ways in which groups responded to the Kodak executives. You can use symbols.

Use the symbol – if groups exhibited low confidence in them. Use the symbol ± for moderate confidence and the symbol + for high confidence. As a final step, explain the bases for the symbols that you selected.

Table 6.2.   Executives Pose Questions to Solve Practical Problems at Kodak

Groups	Response*	Explanation
Journalists		
Business Analysts		

*– Low
 ± Moderate
 + High

Activity 6.3

Textbook publishers designed questions specifically to allay consumer anxiety. How did groups respond?

Table 6.3 identifies two groups: teachers and parents.

Complete the table by indicating the ways in which groups responded to the textbook publishers. You can use symbols.

Use the symbol – if groups exhibited low confidence in them. Use the symbol ± for moderate confidence and the symbol + for high confidence. As a final step, explain the bases for the symbols that you selected.

Table 6.3. Scholastic Publishers Pose Questions to Allay Consumer Anxiety about Textbooks

Groups	Response*	Explanation
Teachers		
Parents		

*– Low
± Moderate
+ High

Activity 6.4

Textbook publishers designed questions specifically to solve practical problems. How did groups respond?

Table 6.4 identifies four groups: teachers, parents, school administrators, and school board members.

Complete the table by indicating the ways in which groups responded to the textbook publishers. You can use symbols.

Use the symbol – if groups exhibited low confidence in them. Use the symbol ± for moderate confidence and the symbol + for high confidence. As a final step, explain the bases for the symbols that you selected.

Table 6.4. Scholastic Publishers Pose Questions to Solve Practical Problems about Textbooks

Groups	Response*	Explanation
Teachers		
Parents		
School Administrators		
School Board Members		

*– Low
 ± Moderate
 + High

Activity 6.5

E-textbook publishers designed questions specifically to allay consumer anxiety. How did groups respond?

Table 6.5 identifies five groups: students, teachers, parents, employers, and politicians.

Complete the table by indicating the ways in which groups responded to the e-textbook publishers. You can use symbols.

Use the symbol – if groups exhibited low confidence in them. Use the symbol ± for moderate confidence and the symbol + for high confidence. As a final step, explain the bases for the symbols that you selected.

Table 6.5. **Scholastic Publishers Pose Questions to Allay Consumer Anxiety about E-Textbooks**

Groups	Response*	Explanation
Students		
Teachers		
Parents		
Employers		
Politicians		

*– Low
± Moderate
+ High

Activity 6.6

E-textbook publishers designed questions specifically to solve practical problems. How did groups respond?

Table 6.6 identifies two groups: school administrators who were cautious about endorsing e-textbooks and teachers who were cautious about endorsing them.

Complete the table by indicating the ways in which groups responded to the e-textbook publishers. You can use symbols.

Use the symbol – if groups exhibited low confidence in them. Use the symbol ± for moderate confidence and the symbol + for high confidence. As a final step, explain the bases for the symbols that you selected.

Table 6.6. Scholastic Publishers Pose Questions to Solve Practical Problems about E-Textbooks

Groups	Response*	Explanation
School Administrators		
Teachers		

*– Low
 ± Moderate
 + High

SUMMARY

Industrialists posed questions to influence investors; they also posed them to solve practical problems. They made an impression on textbook publishers.

HOW MUCH TECHNOLOGY DO TEACHERS NEED?

Pressure to push technology into the classroom without proof of its value has deep roots.

—Matt Richtel, 2011

The current hype is that . . . tablet devices will emerge as a competitive threat to real-life teachers.

—Dennis Berman, 2012

Free access to computers and the Internet is now nearly as important to library patrons as borrowing books.

—Leslie Kaufman, 2013

Some persons asked ethical questions about lawyers. Others asked them about educators.

LAWYER ADVERTISEMENTS

Attorneys at established firms had little difficulty attracting business. They relied on their firms' positive reputations to lure clients.

Novice lawyers envied the ease with which well-known competitors attracted clients. They needed a special tool to compete with them. They looked at the tools that professionals were using in non-legal fields.

The lawyers observed the professionals in medicine, dentistry, finance, insurance, and banking who were using commercial advertisements. They noted that some of them placed advertisements discreetly in pamphlets while others displayed them boldly on billboards.

American Bar Association

Struggling lawyers had information that they wanted to distribute. They wished to share information about the schools at which they had been trained, the skills they had acquired, the courtroom encounters they had won, and even the prices that they charged.

The lawyers who were enthusiastic about ads could not commission them. They realized that the American Bar Association (ABA) had a prohibition against them. They feared that it would disbar them for violating that prohibition.

Lawyers from established firms dominated the ABA. They supported the ban on ads; they feared that their competitors would use them in ways that discredited the profession and undermined the justice system.

Proponents

Two Arizona lawyers needed ads to reach a lucrative segment of the legal market. However, they were intimidated by the ABA's ban.

The lawyers contended that their peers at the established firms had engineered the advertising ban in order to suppress them and other competitors. They made this contention in court; they eventually made it to the Supreme Court. They asked the justices to remove the ban.

The two lawyers were ebullient when the justices ruled in their favor. Empowered by that decision, they began to advertise.

Numerous law firms realized that professional practices in their field were changing. They began to advertise during the 1970s. Some of them eventually were spending millions of dollars on advertising each year (Kennedy, 1995).

The leaders of the ABA changed their minds about advertising. In fact, they agreed to help their members with it. They supplied them with sample ads, marketing guidelines, pertinent court rulings, and advice about ethical issues (American Bar Association, 1978; Center for Professional Responsibility, 2012).

Critics

Some lawyers remained skeptical of advertising. They were sure that their competitors were abusing it. They searched for incidents to confirm this conviction (Goldstein, 1978).

The critics looked for lawyers who exhibited conflicts of interest. They focused on those who had collaborated with police on advertising campaigns.

The critics identified lawyers who had tried to display advertisements within patrol cars. They contended that those lawyers, as well as their police associates, had behaved unethically ("Ethics Commission Vetoes," 2003; Maass, 2009; Treen, 2012; Wood, 2002).

The critics hoped that members of the public would create a ruckus about lawyer advertising. They urged them to replace the ABA prohibition with state restrictions (Donovan, 2007; Margolick, 1993).

SCHOOL COMPUTERS

Computers proliferated during the last decades of the twentieth century. They had an enormous impact on every aspect of society, including employment (Hjorth, Burgess, & Richardson, 2012; Kitchin & Dodge, 2011; Straubhaar, LaRose, & Davenport, 2013).

Proponents

Employers were excited about computers. They noted that they increased worker efficiency. They became strong proponents of computers in schools: they requested that schools develop the skills that students later would need after they had graduated and were working in computer-enhanced jobs (Lucchetti & Philbin, 2012; Schweber, 2012).

Laborers had mixed feelings about computers. On one hand, they appreciated the new jobs that they created; on the other hand, they worried about the current jobs that they eliminated.

Laborers worried about the ways that computers affected their own employment; they also worried about the ways that would affect their children's future employment. They became proponents of computers in schools: they asked the schools to ensure that their children had the skills to procure and progress in computer-enhanced jobs.

The proponents wanted teachers to incorporate electronic devices into instruction. They had specific devices in mind.

The proponents recommended desktop computers. Although they were pleased when teachers placed them in school-wide clusters, they recommended that they place them in every classroom (Lankshear & Knobel, 2011).

Proponents endorsed laptops. They stated that these mobile devices enabled students to be flexible about the locations in which they completed assignments. They added that they also prepared them for the portable digital equipment that they would encounter after they had left school and commenced careers.

Proponents endorsed computerized tablets, such as the iPad. They contended that these lightweight, durable, and simple-to-operate devices enabled students to take notes, read books, make calculations, search the Internet, exchange information with classmates, and communicate with teachers (Hamilton, 2008; Proffitt, 2011).

Proponents urged that computers be used for elementary school instruction. They gave examples of ways to employ them for instruction in reading, writing, mathematics, science, and social studies (Lewin, 2003; McCall, 2011; Michaels, Shouse, & Schweingruber, 2008; Monroe, 2004; Trinkle & Merriman, 2001; Shaywitz, 2003).

Proponents were especially eager to expand the use of computers in high schools. They urged teachers to rely on computer-centered instructional strategies such as those that secondary mathematics and science teachers had developed (Singer, Hilton, & Schweingruber, 2006).

Private Schools   Administrators at elite private schools encouraged teachers to embrace computers. They urged them to integrate them throughout the curriculum. Their teachers responded enthusiastically (Hollander, 2012).

The administrators at one private school supplied all students with personal laptop computers and iPad tablets. They contended that they needed both devices to complete critical academic tasks, such as reading electronic textbooks, submitting homework online, accessing digital library materials, entering data into spreadsheets, taking photos, making videos, and employing databases (Hollander, 2012).

The private school administrators used tuition and fees to cover computer expenses. Although they set them high, they insisted that they needed this money to sustain exemplary computer-centered instruction.

Parents who sent their children to public schools were impressed by the computer-centered instruction that students received at elite private schools. They demanded that their children receive comparable instruction (Gabler, 2012).

Public Schools   Public school teachers used digital technology less than the teachers at private schools. They explained that they were restricted because they did not have enough desktop computers, laptops, or tablets. They urged their school administrators to secure equipment for students to use in their schools and in their homes (Bitter & Pierson, 2002; Ivers & Pierson, 2003).

Many public school administrators did not have the funding to purchase and then maintain computers for all of their students. Although they wanted a permanent solution for this problem, they were willing to settle for an expedient one.

School administrators sometimes prodded their students to bring their own devices to school. They urged them to bring laptop computers, tablets, smartphones, and digital cameras. They had copied this strategy from employers.

Employers had encouraged workers to bring personal electronic devices to jobsites. They described the program with a clever acronym: BYOD (*Bring Your Own e-Device*). They made an impression on school administrators, who started their own BYOD programs (Devaney, 2012).

The scholastic BYOD programs were controversial. Although they solved some problems, they created others. Parents readily discerned the new problems.

Parents noted that students brought devices with which their teachers were unfamiliar and with which they could not give them help. They noted that they brought devices without the software needed to filter inappropriate websites. They added that those who did not have devices in their homes could not bring anything at all (Johnson, 2012).

School administrators acknowledged that the BYOD programs had problems. For this reason, they were pleased when influential organizations endorsed them. They beamed when the national Department of Education endorsed them ("Should Schools Embrace," 2012).

Even ardent proponents recognized the burdensome costs of computers. They acknowledged that the costs stemmed from the equipment itself and also from software, maintenance, auxiliary staffing, and personnel training.

Proponents of computers believed that they had a way for school staffs to subsidize a portion of the costs: they recommended that they switch to less expensive digital textbooks. They explained that the savings from these materials could help fund technology (Calmes & Wyatt, 2013; Giordano, 2012a).

Proponents of computers had still another plan to make the devices affordable. They urged the federal government to subsidize them (Giordano, 2012a).

Critics

Some persons were critical of the amount of money spent on computers. They asked whether some of it should be diverted to other scholastic needs.

The critics realized that influential groups such as parents and businesspersons assigned enormous value to computers. Nonetheless, they suspected that they had misjudged their pedagogical usefulness. They noted that they had misjudged the pedagogical usefulness of earlier technologies such as radios, phonographs, tape recorders, and televisions (Giordano, 2009; Oppenheimer, 2003).

Critics were especially concerned about the impact of computers on scholastic achievement. They were cautious because the earlier technologies had a minimal impact on it (Giordano, 2012a).

Critics claimed that public school teachers who had access to computers underutilized them. They conceded that some of them did not have the training, software, or support personnel that they needed. However, they opined that many simply lacked confidence in the devices (Cuban, 2001; Kessler, 2012; Pflaum, 2004).

Critics warned parents that their children could suffer unanticipated consequences from computers. They worried that they could not be physically fit. They warned that they could exhibit impatience, distractibility, forgetfulness, weak interpersonal skills, and atypical self-concepts (Aboujaoude, 2011; Campbell, 2011; Parker-Pope, 2010; Richtel, 2010; Vamosi, 2011).

Critics warned public school teachers that computers had impoverished the content of the traditional curricula. They contended that they focused students' attention on information that was unlike that which had dominated Western culture for millennia (Lieszkovszky, 2011; Nissenbauma & Walkerb, 1988).

Critics warned school administrators that computers inadvertently might exacerbate their financial problems. They pointed to the problems that they had exacerbated for managers in publishing houses, retail bookstores, and libraries (Cullotta, 2012; Giordano, 2010; Haughney, 2012).

The critics raised numerous questions about the groups that were endorsing school technology. They suspected that some of them had complex ethical conflicts (Barnes & Chozick, 2012; Giordano, 2012a; Perr, 2008; Picciano & Spring, 2013; Richtel, 2011b).

EXAMINING ETHICAL QUESTIONS

Some persons posed ethical questions about lawyers. They inspired persons to ask comparable questions about educators.

Activity 7.1

The persons who were enthusiastic about lawyer advertising highlighted the benefits of this practice. How did groups respond?

Table 7.1 identifies two groups: the lawyers at firms with plentiful clients and those at firms with few clients.

Complete the table by indicating the ways in which groups responded to the lawyer-advertising enthusiasts. You can use symbols.

Use the symbol – if groups detected low conflicts of interest. Use the symbol ± for moderate conflicts and the symbol + for high conflicts among them. As a final step, explain the bases for the symbols that you selected.

You can rely on the information in this chapter, additional information, or the information cited in the references. If you are reading this chapter with colleagues, you can confer with them.

Table 7.1.   Enthusiasts Extol Lawyer Advertising

Groups	Response*	Explanation
Lawyers—Plentiful Clients		
Lawyers—Few Clients		

*– Low
 ± Moderate
 + High

Activity 7.2

Critics of lawyer advertising highlighted the drawbacks of this practice. How did groups respond?

Table 7.2 identifies two groups: the lawyers at firms with plentiful clients and those at firms with few clients.

Complete the table by indicating the ways in which groups responded to the critics of lawyer advertising. You can use symbols.

Use the symbol – if groups detected low conflicts of interest among them. Use the symbol ± for moderate conflicts and the symbol + for high conflicts. As a final step, explain the bases for the symbols that you selected.

Table 7.2.   Critics Decry Lawyer Advertising

Groups	Response*	Explanation
Lawyers—Plentiful Clients		
Lawyers—Few Clients		

*– Low
 ± Moderate
 + High

Activity 7.3

The persons who were enthusiastic about school computers highlighted the benefits of the devices. How did groups respond?

Table 7.3 identifies four groups: teachers at public schools, teachers at well-funded private schools, administrators at public schools, and administrators at well-funded private schools.

Complete the table by indicating the ways in which groups responded to the school computer enthusiasts. You can use symbols.

Use the symbol – if groups detected low conflicts of interest among them. Use the symbol ± for moderate conflicts and the symbol + for high conflicts. As a final step, explain the bases for the symbols that you selected.

Table 7.3. Enthusiasts Extol School Computers

Groups	Response*	Explanation
Teachers—Public Schools		
Teachers—Private Schools		
Administrators—Public Schools		
Administrators—Private Schools		

*– Low
 ± Moderate
 + High

Activity 7.4

The persons who were critical of school computers highlighted the drawbacks of the devices. How did groups respond?

Table 7.4 identifies two groups: public school teachers and public school administrators.

Complete the table by indicating the ways in which groups responded to the critics of school computers. You can use symbols.

Use the symbol – if groups detected low conflicts of interest among them. Use the symbol ± for moderate conflicts and the symbol + for high conflicts. As a final step, explain the bases for the symbols that you selected.

Table 7.4. Critics Decry School Computers

Groups	Response*	Explanation
Teachers		
School Administrators		

*– Low
 ± Moderate
 + High

SUMMARY

Persons examined the groups that advocated professional practices and those that opposed them. They detected conflicts of interest among members of both groups.

8

DO GRADES MATTER?

[The Florida Department of Education] will continue to look for ways to improve the grade calculation process.

—Gerard Robinson, quoted in "Florida Gives," 2012

State educational systems are judged head-to-head largely on the basis of test scores.

—Michael Brick, 2012

If we worked and did well, we got an A. . . . If we goofed off, we got an F. . . . We knew where we stood every day.

—Joseph Korff, quoted in "Common Core," 2013

[Grades] lower self-esteem, discourage creativity, and reinforce the class divide.

—Michael Thomsen, 2013

Reports [in which grades are assigned to schools] help parents . . . understand schools' strengths and weaknesses.

—New York City Schools, 2013

Numerous groups relied on grades. When they were challenged over the ways that they assigned them, they made adaptations.

COLLEGE ADMINISTRATORS

A group of liberal-minded trustees opened Antioch College during the 1850s. They immediately had to decide which students they would allow to enroll at this Ohio institution. They resolved to admit all students, including the females and African Americans who had been banned by most other institutions (Fain, 2007).

The Antioch trustees had to deal with numerous problems. They invited everyone on the campus to help solve them. However, they did not foresee the commotion that this invitation would create (Finnegan, 2010).

Antioch's constituents were unable to discuss problems amicably. They stunned the public when their discussions devolved into protests, boycotts, and strikes (Goldfarb, 2007; Will, 2007).

The Antioch constituents discussed every aspect of the institution, including assessment. They noted that professors were assessing their students by assigning letter grades to them.

Some Antioch faculty members worried that the letter grades might be psychologically harmful to students. They wished to abandon them.

The Antioch administrators may have feared that abandoning grades could create a backlash from employers, parents, and other universities. Nonetheless, they acceded to the faculty.

The administrators continued to keep student records. Unable to represent students' progress with grades, they looked for another way to represent it on those records. They asked the professors to supply descriptive accounts of students' work (Jaschik, 2009).

The administrators came up with a term for their new assessment system: they referred to it as *narrative evaluation*. They felt validated when the staffs at several other colleges endorsed it.

The administrators expected students to embrace their new assessment policy. They were surprised when some of them complained ("Colleges and Universities That Use," 2012).

The students faced practical problems when they applied for the postbaccalaureate programs at other universities. They were required to submit transcripts with grades. They were required to submit them for jobs as well (Maeroff, 1979).

The Antioch students were at a disadvantage when they had to furnish grades. However, they were at a disadvantage even when they had to furnish scores from standardized tests. They discovered that years of nongraded academic studies had dulled their aptitude for the tests.

Students and their parents complained about Antioch's problems. They created anxiety among prospective students and their parents (Donahue, 2011).

The administrators had difficulty recruiting students to Antioch. As a result, they could not collect enough revenue to sustain college operations. They realized that they were in financial peril. Although they promised to change some of their unconventional practices, they worried that they had waited too long (Hannah, 2008).

TEACHERS

Parents had numerous questions for the early teachers. They repeatedly asked about grades: they wanted to know how they were assigned.

Most of the teachers awarded grades on the basis of a single criterion: whether students could recount key information. They assigned A to those who expertly recounted it, B through D to those who inconsistently recounted it, and F to those who could not recount it (Giordano, 2009).

The teachers shared their grades with students. They hoped that high grades would sustain good study habits; they hoped that low grades would change poor study habits.

The teachers also shared grades with parents. They were pleased when they used them to hold children accountable. They were nervous when they used them to hold teachers accountable.

Some parents held teachers accountable for low grades. They protested that they had underestimated bright and hardworking students. They accused them of assigning the wrong grades to them.

Some parents held teachers accountable when they assigned inappropriately high grades to students. They wondered why other teachers would not assign equally high grades to those students.

Parents were not the only group that cared about grades. Employers cared because they used them to screen workers. Military officials cared because they used them to screen soldiers.

Parents, employers, and the military berated the teachers for assigning inaccurate grades. This group became even more formidable after it enlisted allies from higher education and the government (Giordano, 2012b).

The groups that were critical of teachers wanted them to assign grades objectively. They gave them a specific suggestion—rely on standardized testing.

POLITICIANS

President George W. Bush was an unwavering advocate of scholastic testing. He was sure that parents of public school children supported him. He had a detailed national plan to expand testing.

Jeb Bush was the president's brother, the governor of Florida, and another fervent advocate of standardized testing. He was sure that the parents of the public school children in his state supported him. He embraced his brother's plan to expand testing; he then coupled it with an even more ambitious state plan.

Governor Bush made a three-step proposal: enlarge the scope of educational testing, accelerate the schedule for administering tests, and widely publicize the results. He assured constituents that his proposal would raise the profiles of Florida's schools (Madison, 2012; Matus, 2011; Simon, 2012).

Many teachers resisted the call for standardized testing. They resisted partially because of the expense. They were concerned about the cost of the tests as well as the cost of the personnel, administration, utilities, equipment, and facilities that were associated with them.

The cost of standardized scholastic tests increased. It increased because federal and state politicians demanded that the tests be made more sophisticated and administered more frequently (Collins, 2012; Giordano, 2005, 2012a).

Obama Supports Standardized Tests

Assessment enthusiasts were pleased with President Bush and his brother. They were nervous when Barack Obama was competing for the presidency in 2008. They feared that he would win the election and then reduce the priority of educational assessment.

The assessment enthusiasts were relieved after Obama became president but announced that he would continue the Bush-era national testing initiatives. Like Bush, Obama detected strong parental support for greater testing.

The assessment enthusiasts wished to collaborate with Obama. They had a special plan for state tests: they wanted to raise the passing scores on them.

Setting Passing Scores on Tests

A group of Floridians looked at the passing score on their state's fourth-grade writing exam. They concluded that it was too low.

The experts at Pearson Publishing managed the largest educational testing service in America. They had contracts to develop, validate, publish, and score the educational tests in many states. They had contracts for most of the exams in Florida, including the fourth-grade writing exam (Giordano, 2005; "Testing Industry's Big Four," 2002; Way, 2012)

The Pearson experts explained that Florida's fourth-graders could earn scores that ranged from one to six points on the writing exam. They had recommended three points as an ambitious passing score; they predicted that 19 percent of the students would fail to earn this score.

State politicians agreed to the three-point score. They judged that this lofty target would improve instruction.

The Florida politicians resolved that they would use the test scores not only to assess students but also to assess schools. They decided to give the schools grades from A to F. They noted that these were the same grades that the teachers were giving to students ("Database: Florida," 2012; "Florida Gives Wrong Grades," 2012).

Florida's teachers challenged the plan to grade schools on the bases of students' test scores. Although they conceded that schools influenced these scores, they noted that nonscholastic factors also influenced them.

Florida's teachers had another reason to challenge the school-grading plan: they were upset about the passing scores on state tests. They explained that the three-point passing score for the writing test ensured that 19 percent of the fourth-graders would fail. They judged that this proportion was too high.

The Florida teachers had been anxious about the three-point passing score for the writing test; they became even more anxious when that score was raised by another point. They anticipated dramatic changes.

Like the teachers, politicians had anticipated changes. Nonetheless, they were stunned when the Florida Department of Education disclosed the results: the number of students who failed the examination increased from 19 to 73 percent (Campo-Flores, 2012).

Parents did not understand why so many more children had failed the writing exam. They demanded an explanation. They instead received a promise: the previous passing score would be reinstated. In fact, it would be reinstated retroactively (Winerip, 2012).

SCHOOL ADMINISTRATORS

Florida parents were upset when children did not pass tests; they also were upset when they did not pass classes. They expressed their concerns to teachers, many of whom were not sympathetic. They also expressed them to school administrators.

The school administrators sympathized with the parents. They recognized that low grades had a compound influence on children: they affected them immediately in school and then later in colleges and workplaces.

Although the administrators worried about the ways that low grades affected students, they also worried about the ways that they affected schools. They realized that they determined whether schools could project positive public images, attract federal money, secure state funds, and retain talented teachers.

The school administrators had still another reason to be concerned about grades: they could lose their managerial positions if their students' grades were low.

School administrators discussed grading with teachers. They implored them to consider its complex and potentially dire consequences.

The administrators were able to persuade some teachers to change grades. They could not persuade all of them.

Obstinate teachers stated that students could change grades on their own. They explained that they simply had to repeat classes, master the curriculum, and earn higher grades.

The administrators realized that not all students were willing to repeat classes. They looked for a solution to this problem. They hoped to find one that did not require confrontations with hard-nosed teachers.

The administrators eventually did devise an alternative way to change low grades. They allowed students to alter them through online learning activities. They referred to the strategy as *grade recovery*.

The school administrators did not have the staffs to implement grade recovery on their own. They therefore asked commercial vendors to create learning materials, present them online, and monitor students as they progressed through them ("Credit and Grade Recovery," 2011; "Flexible Credit Recovery," 2011; "Grade Recovery Programs," 2011).

Teachers disdained the materials used for grade recovery. They complained that they contained only a portion of the information from their courses.

The administrators acknowledged that the online materials were truncated. They explained that they had been edited so that students could focus on those portions of courses with which they had struggled (Bainbridge, 2007).

The administrators waited to see how high school students responded to grade recovery. They were delighted when more than 30 percent of them took advantage of it in some communities (Sanders, 2011).

EXAMINING DISCRETIONARY QUESTIONS

Teachers, school administrators, professors, and politicians relied on grades. When they were challenged over the procedures for assigning them, they made adjustments.

Activity 8.1

University administrators listened to complaints about the problems that professors faced when they assigned letter grades. They authorized the professors to substitute narrative evaluations for the grades. How did groups respond?

Table 8.1 identifies three groups: university students who were assessed with narrative evaluations, employers, and admissions personnel at those colleges who continued to rely on grades.

Complete the table by indicating the ways in which groups responded to the administrators who authorized narrative evaluations. You can use symbols.

Use the symbol – if groups demonstrated low support for them. Use the symbol ± for moderate support and the symbol + for high support. As a final step, explain the bases for the symbols that you selected.

You can rely on the information in this chapter, additional information, or the information cited in the references. If you are reading this chapter with colleagues, you can confer with them.

Table 8.1. University Administrators Authorize Professors to Use Narrative Evaluations

Groups	Response*	Explanation
Students		
Employers		
Admissions Personnel—Used Grades		

*– Low
± Moderate
+ High

Activity 8.2

Presidents George W. Bush and Obama worried that teachers were assigning inappropriate grades to students. They required them to rely to a greater extent on standardized tests. How did groups respond?

Table 8.2 identifies two groups: teachers in public schools and parents of public school students.

Complete the table by indicating the ways in which groups responded to the two presidents. You can use symbols.

Use the symbol – if groups demonstrated low support for them. Use the symbol ± for moderate support and the symbol + for high support. As a final step, explain the bases for the symbols that you selected.

Table 8.2. Presidents Bush and Obama Require Teachers to Rely More on Standardized Tests

Groups	Response*	Explanation
Teachers		
Parents		

*– Low
± Moderate
+ High

Activity 8.3

Florida politicians received complaints over the high scores that students had to earn in order to pass state-mandated exams. They therefore lowered the passing grades. How did groups respond?

Table 8.3 identifies two groups: teachers in the Florida public schools and the parents of students in those schools.

Complete the table by indicating the ways in which groups responded to the Florida politicians. You can use symbols.

Use the symbol – if groups demonstrated low support for them. Use the symbol ± for moderate support and the symbol + for high support. As a final step, explain the bases for the symbols that you selected.

Table 8.3. Florida Politicians Lower Passing Scores on State-Mandated Exams

Groups	Response*	Explanation
Teachers		
Parents		

*– Low
  ± Moderate
  + High

Activity 8.4

Florida school administrators received complaints about the low grades that teachers were assigning to students. They authorized the students to use grade recovery to raise their grades. How did groups respond?

Table 8.4 identifies four groups in Florida: public school students, parents of public school students, teachers, and the entrepreneurs who marketed online courses.

Complete the table by indicating the ways in which groups responded to the school administrators. You can use symbols.

Use the symbol – if groups demonstrated low support for them. Use the symbol ± for moderate support and the symbol + for high support. As a final step, explain the bases for the symbols that you selected.

Table 8.4. Florida School Administrators Authorize Students to Use Grade Recovery

Groups	Response*	Explanation
Students		
Parents		
Teachers		
Entrepreneurs—Online Courses		

*– Low
± Moderate
+ High

SUMMARY

Teachers, school administrators, professors, and politicians relied on grades. When they were challenged over procedures for assigning them, they developed alternative procedures.

9

WHAT PRODS POLITICIANS TO COLLABORATE ON SCHOOLS?

The typical U.S. public school superintendent tolerates parents, submits to his school board but hates and fears his mayor.

—"Education: Schools and Politics," 1938

If you're a politician who has all kinds of things to say about public education, do voters have the right to know where you send your children to school?

—Matt Bai, 2011

Political campaigns . . . forge ahead with a falsehood if they think it will score . . . points.

—Bill Adair, quoted by Cooper, 2012

We have to realize that [the New York] schools are not an employment program.

—Governor Andrew Cuomo, quoted by Kaplan & Taylor, 2012

Governors . . . are no better suited to run schools than they are to run construction sites.

—P. L. Thomas, 2012

Politicians faced questions about their collaborators. Some were candid when they answered; others were cunning.

CREATIVE COLLABORATIONS

Fabrice Morvan and Rob Pilatus stood out from other singers of the 1980s. They had good looks, charm, impressive musical taste, and incredibly wide vocal ranges.

A German producer gave the young men a clever stage name—*Milli Vanilli*. He then orchestrated public appearances, arranged tours, marketed albums, and helped them procure a Grammy Award.

Three unknown performers created additional publicity for Morvan and Pilatus in 1989. They shocked the public when they disclosed that Morvan and Pilatus had depended on them to perform the vocals on their recordings (Pareles, 1990).

Musicians were not the only persons who depended on collaborators. Many public figures relied on them when they published books. Some of them recruited them from book agents, others from publishers, and still others from the professional association for ghostwriters (Lim, 2012; Moskin, 2012; Turner, 2011).

Politicians were impressed by the ways in which numerous professionals had benefited from books. They judged that they could benefit by authoring books about history, domestic policies, foreign affairs, or their own lives. John F. Kennedy detected these opportunities when he was in Congress.

Kennedy had won a position in the House of Representatives and then later in the Senate. He wished to win a much more prestigious position: he planned to become president.

Kennedy worried that some persons viewed him as intellectually shallow. He hoped to change their views with a history book. He proposed to focus on famous figures in American government.

Kennedy asked his speechwriter, Ted Sorenson, to help him. He was fortunate because Sorenson was an experienced author and a distinguished historian.

Kennedy was pleased to have Sorenson as his collaborator. However, he feared that Sorenson would be viewed as the primary author of the book. He decided to conceal their relationship; he claimed that he had written the book by himself (Adams, 2003).

Kennedy entitled the book *Profiles in Courage.* He was delighted when it sold multiple copies, elicited numerous compliments, and earned a Pulitzer Prize (Kennedy, 1956; Parmet, 1980).

Many politicians were inspired by Kennedy to write their own books. They asked campaign strategists, book agents, or publishers to locate coauthors. They also asked them for advice about whether they should acknowledge or conceal their coauthors (Fehrman, 2010).

Those politicians who acknowledged coauthors took a risk: their own contribution could be denigrated. Those who did not acknowledge them also took a risk: they would appear dishonest if the collaborators were discovered (Sanchez & Weigel, 2008).

EDUCATIONAL COLLABORATIONS

When politicians collaborated on books, some of them highlighted their coauthors. Others hid them. They had to make similar decisions about many of the persons with whom they collaborated.

Mayor-Led School Boards

Aspiring school board members looked for ways to win elections. They asked influential persons to endorse them. They also asked them to provide funding for them. They sometimes attracted high-profile endorsements and millions of dollars (Medina, 2013).

Influential persons viewed the backing they gave to candidates as *quid pro quo.* They expected those candidates who were successful to protect their interests from ambitious mayors.

As for the mayors, they were annoyed when school board members stood up to them. They depicted them as partisan. They announced that they had a plan to make them less partisan: they personally would appoint them.

The mayors argued that appointed school boards would be highly independent. They claimed that they would be more independent than elected boards because they would not be indebted to sponsors. They insisted that they would be able to increase teacher accountability and lower educational spending (Banchero, 2012a; Resmovits, 2010).

Skeptics questioned whether mayor-appointed school boards truly were independent. They highlighted instances in which they had deferred obsequiously to their mayors (Bracey, 2009; Cooper, 2012; Gardner, 2011; Medina, 2009).

Chicago's School Board

The problems in Chicago's public school were complex: they were entwined with housing, transportation, employment, business, organized labor, and politics. They also were longstanding: they had festered for decades.

Chicago's problems regularly received national attention. They attracted an inordinate amount of attention during the 2012 mayoral campaign ("Chicago's Teaching Moment," 2012; Shipps, 2006).

Rahm Emanuel was responsible for some of the attention. He caused a sensation when he resigned as the president's chief of staff to become a mayoral candidate. He campaigned on a pledge to solve Chicago's school problems.

Emanuel stated that he would concentrate on teachers. He explained that the teachers, who were among the highest-paid educators in the country, had failed to help students earn high scores on standardized tests (Banchero, 2012b).

Emanuel had a strategy for placing pressure on teachers. He personally would appoint school board members with backgrounds in business rather than education. He assumed that they would have the experience, knowledge, and courage to stand up to the teachers.

After Emanuel won the election, he appointed his school board members. He then asked them to identify steps to improve the schools.

The board members realized that the mayor already had identified these steps. In fact, he had articulated them throughout the campaign. Nonetheless, they dutifully repeated them (McCune, 2012).

The board highlighted the steps that they needed to take to improve schools. They had to reduce spending on teachers, create more charter schools, eliminate some neighborhood schools, extend the school year, and make test scores more important on teacher evaluations (Banchero & Maher, 2012).

The members of the local teachers union were not asked for recommendations to improve schools. They gave them anyway. They recommended that the school board preserve the current practices for funding teachers' salaries, the current procedures for evaluating teachers' performance, the current restraints on charter schools, the current length for the school year, and the current protections for teachers who lost jobs after school closures (Omer, 2012).

The teachers demanded that the board consider their recommendations. They warned that they would strike if they were ignored. They added that they were prepared to strike at the beginning of the 2012 school year.

The school board members had doubts about the teachers' commitment to children. They had no doubt about their commitment to their salaries and job security. They resolved that they would ignore them and brace for a strike (Banchero & Belkin, 2012; "Union Wins," 2012).

Even though the school board members had anticipated that the teachers would strike, they did not anticipate the way that they would characterize it. They were surprised when the teachers characterized it as an effort to protect children from an excessively political mayor and school board.

The school board members were impressed by the teachers' clever rhetoric. They conceded that it was affecting the manner in which journalists reported about the strike and the ways that parents viewed it. Wishing to engender their own support among these groups, they stated that their commitment to children was greater than that of teachers.

The school board members were only somewhat successful. They were disappointed when journalists and parents continued to accuse them of placing the mayor's political interests ahead of children's scholastic interests (Davey, 2012; Epstein, 2012).

EXAMINING POLITICIZED QUESTIONS

Politicians were asked about the extent to which they depended on collaborators. They were not sure of the best way to respond.

Activity 9.1

Fabrice Morvan and Rob Pilatus secretly collaborated with singers on the *Milli Vanilli* recordings. However, they were unable to conceal their collaboration. How did groups respond?

Table 9.1 identifies three groups: music critics, persons on the Grammy Awards committee, and members of the public.

Complete the table by indicating the ways in which groups responded to the duo's collaboration. You can use symbols.

Use the symbol – if groups exhibited little interest. Use the symbol ± for moderate interest and the symbol + for high interest. As a final step, explain the bases for the symbols that you selected.

You can rely on the information in this chapter, additional information, or the information cited in the references. If you are reading this chapter with colleagues, you can confer with them.

Table 9.1. Morvan and Pilatus Fail to Conceal Collaborators on the *Milli Vanilli* Recordings

Groups	Response*	Explanation
Music Critics		
Grammy Awards Committee		
Members of the Public		

*– Low
 ± Moderate
 + High

Activity 9.2

John F. Kennedy secretly collaborated with an author on *Profiles in Courage*. However, he was unable to conceal their collaboration. How did groups respond?

Table 9.2 identifies three groups: book critics, persons on the Pulitzer Prize committee, and members of the general public.

Complete the table by indicating the ways in which groups responded to Kennedy's collaboration. You can use symbols.

Use the symbol – if groups exhibited little interest. Use the symbol ± for moderate interest and the symbol + for high interest. As a final step, explain the bases for the symbols that you selected.

Table 9.2.   John F. Kennedy Fails to Conceal a Collaborator on *Profiles in Courage*

Groups	Response*	Explanation
Book Critics		
Pulitzer Prize Committee		
Members of the Public		

*– Low
 ± Moderate
 + High

Activity 9.3

Mayor Emanuel secretly collaborated with the members of Chicago's school board. However, he was unable to conceal their collaboration. How did groups respond?

Table 9.3 identifies three groups: unionized teachers, journalists, and the parents of children in the public schools.

Complete the table by indicating the ways in which groups responded to Emanuel's collaboration. You can use symbols.

Use the symbol – if groups exhibited little interest. Use the symbol ± for moderate interest and the symbol + for high interest. As a final step, explain the bases for the symbols that you selected.

Table 9.3. Mayor Emanuel Fails to Conceal Collaborators on Chicago's School Board

Groups	Response*	Explanation
Unionized Teachers		
Journalists		
Parents of Public School Children		

*– Low
 ± Moderate
 + High

SUMMARY

Politicians were asked about the degree to which they depended on collaborators. They did not always respond candidly.

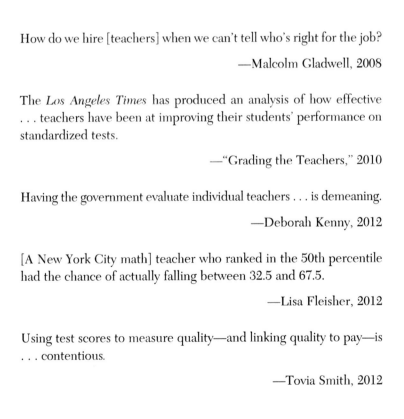

HOW MUCH DATA ON TEACHERS IS NEEDED?

How do we hire [teachers] when we can't tell who's right for the job?

—Malcolm Gladwell, 2008

The *Los Angeles Times* has produced an analysis of how effective . . . teachers have been at improving their students' performance on standardized tests.

—"Grading the Teachers," 2010

Having the government evaluate individual teachers . . . is demeaning.

—Deborah Kenny, 2012

[A New York City math] teacher who ranked in the 50th percentile had the chance of actually falling between 32.5 and 67.5.

—Lisa Fleisher, 2012

Using test scores to measure quality—and linking quality to pay—is . . . contentious.

—Tovia Smith, 2012

Some groups were concerned about retail information; they wished to restrict the public's access to it. Others were concerned about educational information: they wished to expand the public's access to it.

RETAIL PROBLEMS

Best Buy established its first store during the 1960s. It quickly added more. Within a decade, it had assembled an extremely popular and profitable retail chain.

American consumers went to Best Buy stores because of their convenient locations and comprehensive inventories. However, they primarily went for low prices. They eventually were making 15 percent of electronics purchases at these stores (Anderson, 2012).

Executives

Best Buy executives were delighted when business boomed. They were sour when it declined. They asked their stores' managers about the reason for a particularly prolonged decline in 2012.

The managers focused on patrons' attitudes. They noted that the patrons, who originally had been excited by low prices, became less excited as the stores' prices climbed. They reported that they still were visiting the stores, but sometimes only to speak with knowledgeable salespeople and experiment with new products.

The consumers were purchasing more and more products from online retailers. These retailers could keep prices low because they had modest overhead. They also could keep them low because they did not collect sales taxes (Jones, 2012).

The executives listened carefully to the managers; they were convinced that they had isolated the reason for declining sales. They felt vindicated when journalists agreed with them.

The journalists confirmed that some consumers were visiting retail showrooms only to gather information about products. They referred to these consumers as *showroomers* (Zimmerman, 2012a, 2012b).

The executives looked for a way to win back showroomers. They experimented with drive-through lanes at their stores. They hoped that consumers would use these lanes to pick up, return, and pay for the items that they had ordered through the corporate website (Clifford, 2012).

Some business analysts were skeptical of the way that Best Buy's executives had evaluated their problem. They were equally skeptical of their solution for solving that problem.

Skeptics

The skeptical business analysts kept their eyes on the prices of the corporation's stock. They assumed that increasing prices indicated that the executives were handling problems effectively; they assumed that declining prices indicated that they were struggling.

The skeptics became extremely attentive in 2012; they noted that the value of the Best Buy stock was dropping sharply. They were startled when it dropped by more than 40 percent.

The skeptics conceded that a portion of the decline could be attributed to showrooming. They suspected that another portion was the result of executive ineptitude.

The skeptics used a 2007 incident to explain their suspicions of executive ineptitude. They noted that the Best Buy executives had blamed Internet-based shopping for the financial damages that the chain was suffering back then.

The executives came up with a proposal to curb Internet-based shopping. They installed special in-store computers. They encouraged patrons to use them to obtain product information, ascertain prices, and confirm that they were getting good deals.

Consumers soon discovered that the in-store computers did not give them all of the data that they needed. They noted that each computer, which did not link to external websites, displayed information only about items in the particular store where it was situated (Lazarus, 2007).

The executives insisted that they had not deliberately restricted access to data; they stated that they simply had made an oversight. They pledged that they quickly would connect all in-store computers to the company's website.

The executives hoped that persons would be appeased. They were moderately successful in 2007; they were less successful in 2012 (Bustillo, 2012).

EDUCATIONAL PROBLEMS

Politicians were sure that they could solve school problems through legislation. They frequently had to bridge partisan chasms to enact it.

Politicians

George W. Bush proposed the *No Child Left Behind* bill in 2002. He hoped that it would become his signature presidential achievement. However, he needed legislative supporters to enact it.

Bush had no trouble marshaling Republicans; he had difficulty summoning Democrats. He searched for an influential politician to help him. He was delighted when Senator Edward Kennedy volunteered to gather Democrats.

Many parents of public school children were pleased with Bush's education bill. However, others disapproved of the manner in which it expanded educational tests, linked them to federal funding, and publicized their results (Giordano, 2005).

The political sponsors realized that *No Child Left Behind* was contentious. Nonetheless, they were sure that most parents supported it; they also were sure that they wanted to know the scores from scholastic tests.

The journalists in every state were adjured to distribute the scores from federally mandated tests. They complied eagerly.

Journalists in California published aggregated scores for their state, the educational districts in it, and the schools within the districts. Those at the *Los Angeles Times* went further: they published the scores for the individual classrooms in their local schools ("Los Angeles Teacher Ratings," 2010).

Skeptics

Some teachers were skeptical of *No Child Left Behind.* They questioned the tests themselves, the amount of time spent preparing for them, and the manner in which results were publicized (Darling-Hammond, 2012).

The skeptical teachers were agitated by the Los Angeles journalists who published classroom scores. They feared that the teachers in those classrooms would be evaluated on the bases of their scores.

The school administrators who conducted teacher evaluations tried to calm the skeptics. They promised to blend data about students' test scores with other types of data (Kane, 2012).

The skeptics were not reassured. They lamented that connecting teachers to test scores created the perception that the teachers were responsible for those scores. They ticked off a list of numerous other factors that could have been responsible (Giordano, 2005).

One skeptic stated that politicians influenced test scores as much as teachers. She explained that they had influenced them when they mandated increased testing but did not provide increased funding for instruction (Weingarten, 2012).

The skeptical teachers believed that the federal politicians who endorsed testing had conflicts of interests. Nonetheless, they respected their immense power. In fact, they noted that they were using alliances with mayors to amplify their power (Postal, 2011; Watanabe, 2010).

The teachers were particularly wary of Michael Bloomberg, the anti-union mayor of New York City. They anticipated that this influential figure would demand disclosure of classroom test scores. They waited anxiously for his reaction to the Los Angeles classroom disclosures (Santos & Phillips, 2012).

Bloomberg stated that residents of New York City had the same rights as those of Los Angeles. He insisted that these rights had the highest priority. He demanded that his constituents be given the classroom test scores.

The teachers had anticipated the response from Bloomberg. They were surprised by the response from another politician—Arne Duncan, President Obama's secretary of education.

The teachers had overwhelmingly supported Obama during his presidential campaign. They had anticipated that he and his secretary would challenge the link between educational problems and restrictions on classroom testing data.

Duncan did not take the side of the teachers. He predicted that the removal of restrictions on classroom testing data would help solve education problems. He endorsed the release of classroom assessment information by the Los Angeles journalists; he encouraged the release of classroom assessment information in other cities throughout the nation (Song, 2010).

The teachers realized that they needed influential supporters to put pressure on the administration. They asked union leaders, liberal-minded journalists, and sympathetic parents to help them. They cheered when their supporters pressured the secretary of education to reverse his stance on the Los Angeles incident (Santos & Phillips, 2012; Sawchuk, 2012; Shanks, 2012).

EXAMINING PRACTICAL QUESTIONS

Groups contended that access to information created practical problems. Some tried to solve the problems by restricting access; others tried to solve them by expanding it.

Activity 10.1

Best Buy's executives linked retail problems to the public's unrestricted access to data. How did groups respond?

Table 10.1 identifies two groups: journalists and business analysts.

Complete the table by indicating how the groups responded to the executives. You can use symbols.

Use the symbol – if groups exhibited low confidence in them. Use the symbol ± for moderate confidence and the symbol + for high confidence. As a final step, explain the bases for the symbols that you selected.

You can rely on the information in this chapter, additional information, or the information cited in the references. If you are reading this chapter with colleagues, you can confer with them.

Activity 10.2

Best Buy's executives tried to solve retail problems by restricting the public's access to data. How did groups respond?

Table 10.2 identifies two groups: business analysts and showroomers.

Complete the table by indicating how the groups responded to the executives. You can use symbols.

Use the symbol – if groups exhibited low confidence in them. Use the symbol ± for moderate confidence and the symbol + for high confidence. As a final step, explain the bases for the symbols that you selected.

Table 10.1. Best Buy Executives Blame Retail Problems on Public Access to Data

Groups	Response*	Explanation
Journalists		
Business Analysts		

*− Low
  ± Moderate
  + High

Table 10.2. Best Buy's Executives Try to Solve Retail Problems by Restricting Public Access to Data

Groups	Response*	Explanation
Business Analysts		
Showroomers		

*− Low
  ± Moderate
  + High

Activity 10.3

Secretary of Education Duncan linked educational problems to restrictions on public access to classroom testing data. How did groups respond?

Table 10.3 identifies two groups: public school teachers and parents of public school students.

Complete the table by indicating how the groups responded to the secretary of education. You can use symbols.

Use the symbol – if groups exhibited low confidence in him. Use the symbol ± for moderate confidence and the symbol + for high confidence. As a final step, explain the bases for the symbols that you selected.

Table 10.3. Secretary of Education Duncan Links Educational Problems to Restrictions on Classroom Testing Data

Groups	Response*	Explanation
Teachers		
Parents		

*– Low
 ± Moderate
 + High

Activity 10.4

Secretary of Education Duncan initially endorsed the public release of classroom testing data. How did groups respond?

Table 10.4 identifies two groups: public school teachers and parents of public school students.

Complete the table by indicating how the groups responded to the secretary of education. You can use symbols.

Use the symbol – if groups exhibited low confidence in him. Use the symbol ± for moderate confidence and the symbol + for high confidence. As a final step, explain the bases for the symbols that you selected.

Table 10.4. Secretary of Education Duncan Endorses Public Access to Classroom Testing Data

Groups	Response*	Explanation
Teachers		
Parents		

*– Low
± Moderate
+ High

Activity 10.5

Secretary of Education Duncan changed his mind about the public release of classroom testing data; he stated that he opposed it. How did groups respond?

Table 10.5 identifies two groups: public school teachers and parents of public school students.

Complete the table by indicating how the groups responded to the secretary of education. You can use symbols.

Use the symbol – if groups exhibited low confidence in him. Use the symbol ± for moderate confidence and the symbol + for high confidence. As a final step, explain the bases for the symbols that you selected.

Table 10.5. Secretary of Education Duncan Opposes Public Access to Classroom Testing Data

Groups	Response*	Explanation
Teachers		
Parents		

*– Low
± Moderate
+ High

SUMMARY

Groups worried about the ways in which members of the public accessed information. Some of them tried to restrict their access; others tried to increase it.

REFERENCES

Aboujaoude, E. (2011). *Virtually you: The dangerous powers of the e-personality*. New York: Norton.

Adams, C. (2003, November 7). Did John F. Kennedy really write "Profiles in Courage"? Straightdope.com. Retrieved from: http://www.straightdope.com/columns/read/2478/did-john-f-kennedy-really-write-profiles-in-courage.

Adams, S. K., & Baronberg, J. (2005). *Promoting positive behavior: Guidance strategies for early childhood settings*. Upper Saddle River, NJ: Pearson.

Alpert, R. T., Gorth, W. P., & Allan, R. G. (Eds.). (1989). *Assessing basic academic skills in higher education: The Texas approach*. Hillsdale, NJ: Erlbaum.

American Bar Association. (1978). *Lawyer advertising kit: Sample newspaper ads, sample newspaper and magazine articles, sample brochure summarizing legal services, guidance in publicity and promoting legal services*. Chicago: Author.

Anderson, L. (2007). *Congress and the classroom: From the Cold War to "No Child Left Behind."* University Park: Pennsylvania State University Press.

Anderson, M. (2012, August 8). Best Buy founder submits bid to buy the company. *USA Today*. Retrieved from: http://www.usatoday.com/money/industries/retail/story/2012-08-06/best-buy-buyout-schulze/56818360/1.

Anderson, S. (2005, August 25). Teenage wasteland: Farewell to the sadistic pleasures of brat camp. *Slate*. Retrieved from: http://www.slate.com/articles/arts/culturebox/2005/08/teenage_wasteland.html.

As e-book market evolves, correlation between genre preference and device selection is revealed, says new BISG study. (2013, April 5). Bisg.org. Retrieved from: http://www.bisg.org/news-5-827-press-release-as-e-book-market-evolves-correlation-between-genre-prefer-ence-and-device-selection-is-revealed-says-new-bisg-study.php.

Ayers, W., Dohrn, B., & Ayers, R. (Eds.). (2001). *Zero tolerance: Resisting the drive for punishment in our schools: A handbook for parents, students, educators, and citizens*. New York: New Press.

Bai, M. (2011, July 22). On their children's schools, politicians should save the outrage. *New York Times*. Retrieved from: *http://thecaucus.blogs.nytimes.com/2011/07/22/on-their-childrens-schools-politicians-should-save-the-outrage.*

Bainbridge, W. (2007, January 17). Grade recovery can be a positive. *Florida Times-Union*. Retrieved from: http://jacksonville.com/tu-online/stories/011707/opb_baintest.shtml.

Baker, T. (2005). *The medical malpractice myth*. Chicago: University of Chicago Press.

Banchero, S. (2012a, February 23). Chicago shake-up targets 17 schools. *Wall Street Journal*. Retrieved from: http://online.wsj.com/article/SB10001424052970204778604577239643010165010.html.

Banchero, S. (2012b, September 11). In Chicago, standoff built over two years. *Wall Street Journal*. Retrieved from: http://online.wsj.com/article/SB10000872396390443696604577645970141619612.html.

Banchero, S., & Belkin, D. (2012, September 16). Union votes to keep striking. *Wall Street Journal*. Retrieved from: http://online.wsj.com/article/SB10000872396390444500045780004401169588344.html.

Banchero, S., & Maher, K. (2012, September 10). Strike puts spotlight on teacher evaluation, pay. *Wall Street Journal*. Retrieved from: http://online.wsj.com/article/SB1000087239639044392150457764362663814724.html.

Banks, G. W. (2008). *Back to the basics: A holistic approach to correcting the stewardship crisis in the African American church*. Tucson, AZ: Wheatmark.

Barlyn, S., & Vlastelica, R. (2012, May 22). SEC, FINRA to review Facebook issues, Nasdaq sued. Reuters.com. Retrieved from: http://www.reuters.com/article/2012/05/22/us-usa-markets-facebook-idUS-BRE84L0PE20120522.

Barnes, B., & Chozick, A. (2012, August 19). Media companies, seeing profit slip, push into education. *New York Times*. Retrieved from: http://www.nytimes.com/2012/08/20/technology/discovery-invests-in-digital-textbooks-in-hopes-of-growth.html.

Bear, G. G. (2010). *School discipline and self-discipline: A practical guide to promoting prosocial student behavior*. New York: Guilford.

Belch, G. E., & Belch, M. A. (2012). *Advertising and promotion: An integrated marketing communications perspective*. New York: McGraw-Hill.

Berman, D. K. (2012, October 23). In the future, who will need teachers? *Wall Street Journal*. Retrieved from: http://online.wsj.com/article/SB10001424052970203400604578075080640810820.html.

Bialik, C. (2009, October 14). New research on spanking might need a time out. *Wall Street Journal*. Retrieved from: http://online.wsj.com/article/SB125548136491383915.html.

Bilton, N. (2012, June 26). Tech companies announce 'Girls Who Code' initiative. *New York Times*. Retrieved from: http://bits.blogs.nytimes.com/2012/06/26/tech-companies-announce-girls-who-code-initiative.

Bitensky, S. H. (2006). *Corporal punishment of children: A human rights violation*. Ardsley, NY: Transnational.

Bitter, G. G., & Pierson, M. (2002). *Using technology in the classroom*. Boston, MA: Allyn & Bacon.

Boaler, J. (2008). *What's math got to do with it?: Helping children learn to love their most hated subject—and why it's important for America*. New York: Viking.

Boarding School Discipline. (1873, October 11). *New York Times*. Retrieved from: http://select.nytimes.com/gst/abstract.html.

Bosman, J., & Peters, J. W. (2011, September 18). In e-books, publishers have rivals: News sites. *New York Times*. Retrieved from: http://

www.nytimes.com/2011/09/19/business/media/in-e-books-publishing-houses-have-a-rival-in-news-sites.html.

Bowen, S. H. (2010). Discipline in school: What works and what doesn't? Eduguide.org. Retrieved from: http://www.eduguide.org/library/viewarticle/553.

Boyles, D. (Ed.). (2005). *Schools or markets? Commercialism, privatization, and school-business partnerships*. Mahwah, NJ: Erlbaum.

Bracey, G. (2009, July 21). Mayoral control of schools: The new tyranny. *Huffington Post*. Retrieved from: http://www.huffingtonpost.com/gerald-bracey/mayoral-control-of-school_b_240487.html.

Bradley, L. H. (2004). *Curriculum leadership: Beyond boilerplate standards*. Lanham, MD: Scarecrow Education.

Brick, M. (2012, November 12). When "grading" is degrading. *New York Times*. Retrieved from: http://www.nytimes.com/2012/11/23/opinion/grading-schools-isnt-the-answer-its-the-problem.html.

Brickman, P., Coates, D., & Janoff-Bulman, R. (1978). Lottery winners and accident victims: Is happiness relative? *Journal of Personality and Social Psychology*. 36 (8), 917–27.

Brush, F. R., & Black, A. H. (1971). *Aversive conditioning and learning*. New York: Academic Press.

Bryce Harper's retort goes viral. (2012, June 13). Foxsports.com. Retrieved from: http://msn.foxsports.com/mlb/story/washington-nationals-phenom-bryce-harper-clown-question-retort-goes-viral-061312.

Burke, L., & Marshall, J. (2010, May 21). Why national standards won't fix American education: Misalignment of power and incentives. Heritage Foundation. Retrieved from: http://www.heritage.org/research/reports/2010/05/why-national-standards-won-t-fix-american-education-misalignment-of-power-and-incentives.

Business Roundtable. (2007, March 21). *American innovation proclamation*. Author. Retrieved from: http://businessroundtable.org/studies-and-reports/american-innovation-proclamation.

Bussey, J. (2012a, January 4). Kodak's long, slow slide. *Wall Street Journal*. Retrieved from: http://online.wsj.com/article/SB10001424052970203471004577141223745435682.html.

Bussey, J. (2012b, January 13). The anti-Kodak: How a U.S. firm innovates and thrives. *Wall Street Journal*. Retrieved from: http://online.wsj.com/article/SB10001424052970203721704577157001419477034.html.

Bustillo, M. (2012, April 10). Best Buy CEO quits in probe. *Wall Street Journal*. Retrieved from: http://online.wsj.com/article/SB1000142405 27023038154045773355551794808074.html.

California business, education, civic leaders converge at STEM education summit to catalyze California's 21st century workforce. (2012, October 11). Prweb.com. Retrieved from: http://www.prweb.com/releases/2012/10/prweb10002556.htm.

Calmes, J., & Wyatt, E. (2013, June 6). Obama promises to have high-speed internet in most schools in 5 years. *New York Times*. Retrieved from: http://www.nytimes.com/2013/06/07/us/politics/obama-to-seek-more-internet-aid-for-schools-and-libraries.

Campbell, B. A., & Church, R. M. (1969). *Punishment and aversive behavior*. New York: Appleton-Century-Crofts.

Campbell, D. (2011, May 21). Children growing weaker as computers replace outdoor activity. *Guardian*. Retrieved from: http://www.guardian.co.uk/society/2011/may/21/children-weaker-computers-re-place-activity.

Campo-Flores, A. (2012, May 18). Regraded test upends Florida schools. *Wall Street Journal*. Retrieved from: http://online.wsj.com/article/SB10001424052702303879604577412582163862906.html.

Carnoy, M., Elmore, R. F., & Siskin, L. S. (2003). *The new accountability: High schools and high stakes testing*. New York: RoutledgeFalmer.

Carr, S. (2012, May 22). Do "zero tolerance" school discipline policies go too far? *Time*. Retrieved from: http://www.time.com/time/nation/article/0,8599,2115402,00.html.

Cary, M. K. (2012, June 15). Barack Obama's economic speech flops. Usnews.com. Retrieved from: http://www.usnews.com/opinion/blogs/mary-kate-cary/2012/06/15/barack-obamas-economic-speech-flops.

Catalanello, R. (2010, June 2). Textbooks ditched at Clearwater High as students log on to Kindles. *Tampa Bay Times*. Retrieved from: http://www.tampabay.com/news/education/k12/textbooks-ditched-at-clearwater-high-as-students-log-on-to-kindles/1099264.

Center for Professional Responsibility. (2012). Information on professionalism & ethics in lawyer advertising. American Bar Association. Retrieved from: http://www.americanbar.org/groups/professional_responsibility/resources/professionalism/professionalism_ethics_in_lawyer_advertising.html.

Chaltain, S. (2012, July 5). What makes a great school? Forbes.com. Retrieved from: http://www.forbes.com/sites/ashoka/2012/07/05/what-makes-a-great-school.

Charteris-Black, J. (2005). *Politicians and rhetoric: The persuasive power of metaphor.* Houndmills, UK: Palgrave Macmillan.

Chen, B. X., & Bosman, J. (2013, June 2). E-book antitrust trial of Apple to begin. *New York Times.* Retrieved from: http://www.nytimes.com/2013/06/03/technology/e-book-antitrust-case-against-apple-to-begin.html.

Cheney, L. (1997, September 29). A failing grade for Clinton's national standards. *Wall Street Journal.* Retrieved from: http://mathematicallycorrect.com/wsj929.htm.

Chicago's teaching moment. (2012, September 11). *Wall Street Journal.* Retrieved from: http://online.wsj.com/article/SB10000872396390443921504577643401868728684.html.

Clifford, S. (2012, July 4). Luring online shoppers offline. *Wall Street Journal.* Retrieved from: http://www.nytimes.com/2012/07/05/business/retailers-lure-online-shoppers-offline.html.

Colleges and universities that use narrative evaluations. (2012). K12academics.com. Retrieved from: http://www.k12academics.com/education-assessment-evaluation/narrative-evaluation/colleges-universities-use-narrative-evaluations.

Collins, G. (2012, April 27). A very pricey pineapple. *New York Times.* Retrieved from: http://www.nytimes.com/2012/04/28/opinion/collins-a-very-pricey-pineapple.html.

Common core curriculum fails to persuade many. (2013, May 10). *Wall Street Journal* [U.S. Edition]. A14.

Conner, E., Chadwick-Joshua, J., Parks, G. P., Truscott, R. B., & Wajngurt, C. (2012). THEA: Texas Higher Education Assessment. Piscataway, NJ: Research & Education Association.

Cooper, M. (2012, August 31). Campaigns play loose with truth in a fact-check age. *New York Times.* Retrieved from: http://www.nytimes.com/2012/09/01/us/politics/fact-checkers-howl-but-both-sides-cling-to-false-ads.html.

Cordero-Moss, G. (2011). *Boilerplate clauses, international commercial contracts and the applicable law.* Cambridge: Cambridge University Press.

Cornog, E. (2004). *The power and the story: How the crafted presidential narrative has determined political success from George Washington to George W. Bush*. New York: Penguin.

Cost of Edwards' haircut hits $1,250. (2009, February 11). Cbsnews.com. Retrieved from: http://www.cbsnews.com/2100-250_162-3019277.html.

Cowan, L. (2012a, May 22). Facebook slides amid roadshow questions. *Wall Street Journal*. Retrieved from: http://online.wsj.com/article/SB10001424052702304019404577419911507532738.html.

Cowan, L. (2012b, July 20). Two tech IPOs shine following Facebook. *Wall Street Journal*. Retrieved from: http://online.wsj.com/article/SB10000872396390444464304577538810820226638.html.

Credit and grade recovery. (2011). Compasslearning.com. Retrieved from: http://compasslearning.com/Products/show.aspx?page=2.12.0.

Cuban, L. (2001). *Oversold and underused: Computers in the classroom*. Cambridge, MA: Harvard University Press.

Cullotta, K. A. (2012, December 27). Libraries see opening as bookstores close. *New York Times*. Retrieved from: http://www.nytimes.com/2012/12/28/us/libraries-try-to-update-the-bookstore-model.html.

Cummings, C. B. (2000). *Winning strategies for classroom management*. Alexandria, VA: Association for Supervision and Curriculum Development.

Curwin, R. L., Mendler, A. N., & Mendler, B. D. (2008). *Discipline with dignity: New challenges, new solutions*. Alexandria, VA: Association for Supervision and Curriculum Development.

Dahl, M. (2012, November 28). Can $500 million make you happy? Not really. Nbcnews.com. Retrieved from: http://vitals.nbcnews.com/_news/2012/11/28/15463411-can-500-million-make-you-happy-not-really?lite.

Damon, W. (Ed.). (2002). *Bringing in a new era in character education*. Stanford, CA: Hoover Institution Press.

Darling-Hammond, L. (2012, June 24). No: Teaching is too complex. *Wall Street Journal*. Retrieved from: http://online.wsj.com/article/SB10001424052702304723304577366023832205042.html.

Database: Florida school grades 2012. (2012). *Orlando Sentinel*. Retrieved from: http://databases.sun-sentinel.com/news/education/orlandoSchoolGrades2012/ftlaudSchoolGrades_list.php.

Davey, M. (2012, September 10). Teachers' strike in Chicago tests mayor and union. *New York Times*. Retrieved from: http://www. nytimes.com/2012/09/11/education/teacher-strike-begins-in-chicago-amid-signs-that-deal-isnt-close.html.

De Dora, M. (2010, August 17). On what should politicians base their decisions? Blogspot.com. Retrieved from: http://rationally-speaking.blogspot.com/2010/08/on-what-should-politicians-base-their.html.

Debunking the myths. (2012). Justice.org. Retrieved from: http://www. justice.org/cps/rde/xchg/justice/hs.xsl/2011.htm.

Demarest, G. (2011). *Winning insurgent war: Back to basics*. Fort Leavenworth, KS: Foreign Military Studies Office.

Devaney, L. (2012, November 14). How to make BYOD work for your schools. Eschoolnews.com. Retrieved from: http://www.eschoolnews. com/2012/10/29/how-to-make-byod-work-for-your-schools.

Device that changed everything is now changing the classroom. (2012). Apple.com. Retrieved from: http://www.apple.com/education/ipad.

Donahue, B. (2011, September 16). Can Antioch College return from the dead again? *New York Times*. Retrieved from: http://www. nytimes.com/2011/09/18/magazine/can-antioch-college-return-from-the-dead-again.html.

Donnelly, M., & Straus, M. A. (2005). *Corporal punishment of children in theoretical perspective*. New Haven, CT: Yale University Press.

Donovan, K. (2007, March 2). New York law firms struggle with new restrictions on advertising. *New York Times*. Retrieved from: http:// www.nytimes.com/2007/03/02/business/media/02law.html.

Drew, D. E. (2011). *STEM the tide: Reforming science, technology, engineering, and math education in America*. Baltimore: Johns Hopkins University Press.

Dunlap, D. W. (1990, September 9). Sifting through the boilerplate for essentials in a prospectus. *New York Times*. Retrieved from: http:// www.nytimes.com/1990/09/09/realestate/guide-for-home-buyers-sellers-renters-sifting-through-boilerplate-for-essentials.html.

Duval County Public Schools. (2010). Duval virtual instruction academy. Duvalschools.org. Retrieved from: http://www.duvalschools.org/static/ourschools/listings/virtual_school.

Education: Schools and politics. (1938, September 19). *Time*. Retrieved from: http://www.time.com/time/magazine/article/0,9171,931742,00. html#ixzz2V5jRNMoS.

Ellis, G., Morgan, N. S., & Reid, K. (2013). *Better behaviour through home-school relations: Using values-based education to promote positive learning*. New York: Routledge.

Emmer, E. T., Evertson, C. M., Worsham, M. E., & Emmer, E. T. (2006). *Classroom management for middle and high school teachers*. Boston: Pearson.

Engleman, E. (2009, December 19). When "digital" shouldn't mean "cheap." Portfolio.com. Retrieved from: http://www.portfolio.com/ views/blogs/the-tech-observer/2009/12/19/simon-schuster-chief-slams-cheap-ebooks/#ixzz1KBNLZhrU.

Epstein, J. (2012, September 12). Striking teachers, divided antipathies. *Wall Street Journal*. Retrieved from: http://online.wsj.com/article/SB 10000872396390444017504577646123289219502.html.

Ethics commission vetoes ads on patrol cars. (2003, July 11). Legal-weblog.blogspot.com. Retrieved from: http://legalweblog.blogspot. com/2003/07/ethics-commission-vetoes-ads-on-patrol.html.

Evertson, C. M., & Weinstein, C. S. (2006). *Handbook of classroom management: Research, practice, and contemporary issues*. Mahwah, NJ: Erlbaum.

Eviatar, D. (2009, August 19). Tort reform unlikely to cut health care costs. *Washington Independent*. Retrieved from: http://washingtonindependent.com/55535/tort-reform-unlikely-to-cut-health-care-costs.

Fabricant, M., & Fine, M. (2012). *Charter schools and the corporate makeover of public education: What's at stake?* New York: Teachers College.

Fain, P. (2007, June 22). Antioch's closure signals the end of an era. *Chronicle of Higher Education*. Retrieved from: http://chronicle.com/ article/Antioch-s-Closure-Signals-the/4921.

Farber, M. A. (1969, August 17). Survey finds public concerned that discipline in schools is lax. *New York Times*. Retrieved from: http:// select.nytimes.com/gst/abstract.html?res=F40D14FB3B5E1A7B93C 5A81783D85F4D8685F9.

Fehrman, C. (2010, May 23). Ghostwriting and the political book culture. *Los Angeles Times*. Retrieved from: http://articles.latimes. com/2010/may/23/opinion/la-oe-fehrman-ghost-20100523.

Finnegan, L. (2010, May 24). The top non-traditional colleges. *Huffington Post*. Retrieved from: http://www.huffingtonpost.com/2010/05/20/the-top-non-traditional-c_n_584115.html.

Fiske, E. B. (1988, June 8). Schools' back-to-basics drive found to be working in math. *New York Times*. Retrieved from: http://www.nytimes.com/1988/06/08/us/schools-back-to-basics-drive-found-to-be-working-in-math.html.

Flegenheimer, M. (2012, June 19). With speed-camera bill, more writing of tickets may be going hands-free. *New York Times*. Retrieved from: http://www.nytimes.com/2012/06/20/nyregion/in-new-york-cameras-to-catch-speeders-may-arrive-soon.html.

Fleisher, L. (2012, February 25). Wide variations spark skepticism. *Wall Street Journal*. Retrieved from: http://online.wsj.com/article/SB10001424052970203918304577243690477706160.html.

Fleisher, L. (2013, May 17). Where do the mayoral candidates stand on arts education? *New York Times*. Retrieved from: http://blogs.wsj.com/metropolis/2013/05/17/where-do-the-mayoral-candidates-stand-on-arts-education.

Flexible credit recovery solution for grades 5–12. (2011). Keystonecreditrecovery.com. Retrieved from: http://keystonecreditrecovery.com/how-it-works.

Florida gives wrong grades to hundreds of public schools, challenge accountability. (2012, July 24). *Huffington Post*. Retrieved from: http://www.huffingtonpost.com/2012/07/24/florida-gives-wrong-grade_n_1699230.html.

Gabler, N. (2012, January 20). One percent education. *New York Times*. Retrieved from: http://www.nytimes.com/2012/01/22/education/edlife/one-percent-education.html.

Gabrielson, F. H., & Kahn, E. J. (1949, May 14). The talk of the town—Education. *New Yorker*. Retrieved from: http://www.newyorker.com/archive/1949/05/14/1949_05_14_021_TNY_CARDS_000218175#ixzz1h08gweIG.

Gammeltoft, N., & McCormick, J. (2010, August 31). Strayer leads education stocks down as senator proposes curbs on practices. Bloomberg.com. Retrieved from: http://www.bloomberg.com/news/2010-08-31/strayer-leads-education-stocks-down-as-senator-proposes-curbs-on-practices.html.

Gardner, W. (2011, September 9). Mayoral control of schools shows mixed results. *Education Week*. Retrieved from: http://blogs.edweek. org/edweek/walt_gardners_reality_check/2011/09/mayoral_control_ of_schools_shows_mixed_results.html.

Gass, J., & Chieppo, C. (2013, May 27). Common core education is uncommonly inadequate. *Wall Street Journal*. Retrieved from: http:// online.wsj.com/article/SB10001424127887324659404578503561386 927962.html.

Gawande, A. (2009, June). The cost conundrum: What a Texas town can teach us about health care. *New Yorker*. Retrieved from: http://www. newyorker.com/reporting/2009/06/01/090601fa_fact_gawande.

Geography Education Standards Project. (1994). *Geography for life: National geography standards 1994*. Washington, DC: National Geographic Research & Exploration.

Gerdy, J. R. (2000). *Sports in school: The future of an institution*. New York: Teachers College Press.

Giordano, G. (2000). *Twentieth-century reading education: Understanding practices of today in terms of patterns of the past*. London, UK: Elsevier/JAI Press.

Giordano, G. (2003). *Twentieth-century textbook wars: A history of advocacy and opposition*. New York: Peter Lang.

Giordano, G. (2004). *Wartime schools: How World War II changed American education*. New York: Peter Lang.

Giordano, G. (2005). *How testing came to dominate American schools: The history of educational assessment*. New York: Peter Lang.

Giordano, G. (2007). *American special education: A history of early political advocacy*. New York: Peter Lang.

Giordano, G. (2009). *Solving education's problems effectively: A guide to using the case method*. Lanham, MD: Rowman & Littlefield.

Giordano, G. (2010). *Cockeyed education: A case method primer*. Lanham, MD: Rowman & Littlefield.

Giordano, G. (2011). *Lopsided school: Case method briefings*. Lanham, MD: Rowman & Littlefield.

Giordano, G. (2012a). *Capping costs: Putting a price tag on school reform*. Lanham, MD: Rowman & Littlefield.

Giordano, G. (2012b). *Teachers go to rehab: Historical and current advice to instructors*. Lanham, MD: Rowman & Littlefield.

Gladwell, M. (2008, December 15). Most likely to succeed. *New Yorker*. Retrieved from: http://www.newyorker.com/reporting/2008/12/15/081215fa_fact_gladwell.

Gleick, J. (2011). *The information: A history, a theory, a flood*. New York: Pantheon.

Goals 2000: Educate America Act. (1994, March 31). U.S. Government. P. L. No. 103-227., 103rd Congress. Retrieved from: http://www2.ed.gov/legislation/GOALS2000/TheAct/index.html.

Goals of a Montessori school. (2009). Montessoriconnections.com. Retrieved from: http://www.montessoriconnections.com/aboutmontessoried4.html.

Goldfarb, M. (2007, June 17). Where the arts were too liberal. *New York Times*. Retrieved from: http://www.nytimes.com/2007/06/17/opinion/17goldfarb.html.

Goldstein, D. (2011, August 3). Matt Damon, Arne Duncan and the divisive teacher-quality debate. *The Nation*. Retrieved from: http://www.thenation.com/blog/162558/matt-damon-arne-duncan-and-divisive-teacher-quality-debate.

Goldstein, T. (1978, December 29). Business and the law: Mixed effects of lawyer ads. *New York Times*. Retrieved from: http://query.nytimes.com/mem/archive/pdf?res=F2071FFE345413728DDDA00A94DA415B888BF1D3.

Goleman, D., & Norris, G. (2010, April 4). How green is my iPad? *New York Times*. Retrieved from: http://www.nytimes.com/interactive/2010/04/04/opinion/04opchart.html.

Goodman, A. (2012, July 11). Why is Romney running for president? *Commentary*. Retrieved from: http://www.commentarymagazine.com/2012/07/11/why-is-romney-running-for-president-campaign-vision.

Gordon, M. (2012, October 25). Group of 80 CEOs urges tax hikes, spending cuts. *Seattle Times*. Retrieved from: http://seattletimes.com/html/businesstechnology/2019521089_apusceosreducingthedeficit.html.

Gould, M. (2007, January 8). Sparing the rod. *Guardian*. Retrieved from: http://www.guardian.co.uk/education/2007/jan/09/schools.uk1.

Grace, G. R. (2002). *Catholic schools: Mission, markets and morality*. London: Routledge.

Grade recovery programs. (2011). Eduss.com. Retrieved from: http://eduss.com/learning-programs/grade-recovery-programs.

Grading the teachers: Value-added analysis. (2010). *Los Angeles Times* [local edition]. Retrieved from: http://www.latimes.com/news/local/teachers-investigation.

Greene, J. P. (2012, June 22). Let progress trickle up. *Wall Street Journal*. Retrieved from: http://online.wsj.com/article/SB1000142405297 020460300457726923105886366161.html.

Greenfield, J. (2012, April 18). Consumers upset and confused over e-book pricing. Digitalbookworld.com. Retrieved from: http://www.digitalbookworld.com/2012/consumers-upset-and-confused-over-e-book-pricing.

Gregoriou, G. N. (Ed.). (2006). *Initial public offerings: An international perspective*. Oxford, UK: Butterworth-Heinemann.

Hamilton, J. (Ed.). (2008). *Electronic devices in schools*. Detroit: Greenhaven.

Hannah, J. (2008, July 11). Antioch faculty to keep teaching as school closes. *USA Today*. Retrieved from: http://www.usatoday.com/news/nation/2008-07-11-25251221_x.htm.

Haughney, C. (2012, October 22). Young people frequent libraries, study finds. *New York Times*. Retrieved from: http://mediadecoder.blogs.nytimes.com/2012/10/22/young-people-frequent-libraries-study-finds.

Henninger, D. (2012, September 5). Obama speaks. *Wall Street Journal*. Retrieved from: http://online.wsj.com/article/SB1000087239639 04442737045777633622434051452.html.

Hjorth, L., Burgess, J., & Richardson, I. (2012). *Studying mobile media: Cultural technologies, mobile communication, and the iPhone*. New York: Routledge.

Hoffman, J. (2011, December 30). Health groups and school districts are using Web sites and texts to reach teenagers. *New York Times*. Retrieved from: http://www.nytimes.com/2011/12/31/us/sex-education-for-teenagers-online-and-in-texts.html.

Hollander, S. (2012, November 18). Private school goes all in with tech. *Wall Street Journal*. Retrieved from: http://online.wsj.com/article/SB 10001424127887323353204578127104047173928.html.

Howard, P. K. (2009, July 31). Medical tort reform could save billions. *Washington Post*. Retrieved from: http://www.washingtonpost.com/wp-dyn/content/article/2009/07/30/AR2009073002816.html.

Howard, P. N. (2006). *New media campaigns and the managed citizen*. Cambridge, UK: Cambridge University Press.

Hu, W. (2010, June 13). Studying engineering before they can spell. *New York Times*. Retrieved from: http://www.nytimes.com/2010/06/14/education/14engineering.html.

Hu, W. (2011, January 4). Math that moves: Schools embrace the iPad. *New York Times*. Retrieved from: http://www.nytimes.com/2011/01/05/education/05tablets.html.

Huffman, D., & Lawrenz, F. P. (Eds.). (2006). *Critical issues in STEM evaluation*. San Francisco: Jossey-Bass.

Hunt, T. C., Joseph, E. A., & Nuzzi, R. J. (Eds.). (2001). *Handbook of research on Catholic education*. Westport, CN: Greenwood.

In rambling attack, Eastwood targets lawyers at GOP convention. (2012, August 31). Legaltimes.typepad.com. Retrieved from: http://legal-times.typepad.com/blt/2012/08/in-rambling-attack-eastwood-targets-lawyers-at-gop-convention.html.

IRA/NCTE Joint Task Force on Assessment. (1994). *Standards for the assessment of reading and writing*. Newark, DE: International Reading Association.

Is your child happy in school? (2012). K12.com. Retrieved from: http://zsem.k12.com/tpages/tb/paperclip.html.

Ivers, K. S., & Pierson, M. (2003). *A teacher's guide to using technology in the classroom*. Westport, CT: Libraries Unlimited.

Jacobs, A. (2011). *The pleasures of reading in an age of distraction*. New York: Oxford University Press.

Jaschik, S. (2009, January 22). Imagining college without grades. Insidehighered.com. Retrieved from: http://www.insidehighered.com/news/2009/01/22/grades.

John Edwards reduced to Supercuts haircuts. (2012, April 17). *Huffington Post*. Retrieved from: http://www.huffingtonpost.com/2012/04/17/john-edwards-supercuts-_n_1431337.html.

Johnson, C. A. (2009, February 11). Red light cameras stir controversy. Cbsnews.com. Retrieved from: http://www.cbsnews.com/2100-500202_162-2381713.html.

Johnson, C. C. (Ed.). (2011). *Secondary STEM educational reform*. New York: Palgrave Macmillan.

Johnson, D. C. (2003, October 1). The attack on trial lawyers and tort law. Commonweal Institute. Retrieved from: http://www.commonwealinstitute.org/archive/the-attack-on-trial-lawyers-and-tort-law.

Johnson, P. (2012, September 11). BYOD in school not as easy as ABC. *IT World*. Retrieved from: http://www.itworld.com/it-consumerization/294563/byod-school-not-easy-abc.

Jones, A. (2012, January 23). When lawyers become "trolls." *Wall Street Journal*. Retrieved from: http://online.wsj.com/article/SB10001424052970203750404577173402442681284.html.

Jones, R. (2012, July 5). Best Buy, other big retailers fighting back against "showrooming." Msnbc.msn.com. Retrieved from: http://online.wsj.com/article/SB10001424052702303815404577335551794808074.html.

Kafka, J. (2011). *The history of "zero tolerance" in American public schooling*. New York: Palgrave Macmillan.

Kalb, D., Peters, G., & Woolley, J. T. (2007). *State of the union: Presidential rhetoric from Woodrow Wilson to George W. Bush*. Washington, DC: CQ Press.

Kane, T. (2012, June 24). Yes: As one of several measures. *Wall Street Journal*. Retrieved from: http://online.wsj.com/article/SB10001424052702304723304577366023832205042.html.

Kaplan, T., & Taylor, K. (2012, January 16). Invoking King, Cuomo and Bloomberg stoke fight on teacher review impasse. *New York Times*. Retrieved from: http://www.nytimes.com/2012/01/17/nyregion/cuomo-and-bloomberg-on-attack-on-teacher-evaluations.html.

Karlgaard, R. (2012, January 14). Kodak didn't kill Rochester—It was the other way around. *Wall Street Journal*. Retrieved from: http://online.wsj.com/article/SB10001424052970204124204577153053662634584.html.

Kaufman, L. (2013, January 2). Survey finds rising reliance on libraries as a gateway to the web. *New York Times*. Retrieved from: http://mediadecoder.blogs.nytimes.com/2013/01/22/pew-survey-finds-reliance-on-libraries-for-computers-and-internet/?partner=rss&emc=rss.

Kazdin, A. E. (1977). *The token economy: A review and evaluation*. New York: Plenum.

Kennedy, J. F. (1956). *Profiles in courage*. New York: Harper.

Kennedy, R. (1995, May 12). Groundbreaking law firm shifts its focus to personal-injury cases. *New York Times*. Retrieved from: http://www.nytimes.com/1995/05/12/us/groundbreaking-law-firm-shifts-its-focus-to-personal-injury-cases.html.

Kenny, D. (2012, October 14). Want to ruin teaching? Give ratings. *New York Times*. Retrieved from: http://www.nytimes.com/2012/10/15/opinion/want-to-ruin-teaching-give-ratings.html.

Kessler, S. (2012, January 20). Why the iPad won't transform education just yet. Cnn.com. Retrieved from: http://www.cnn.com/2012/01/20/tech/innovation/ipad-wont-transform-education/index.html.

KIPP Foundation. (2013). Kipp.org. Retrieved from: http://www.kipp.org/about-kipp/the-kipp-foundation.

Kitchin, R., & Dodge, M. (2011). *Code/space: Software and everyday life*. Cambridge, MA: MIT Press.

Klein, D. (2002). *A brief history of American K–12 mathematics education in the 20th century*. Csun.edu. Retrieved from: http://www.csun.edu/~vcmth00m/AHistory.html.

Kline, M. (1973). *Why Johnny can't add: The failure of the new math*. New York: St. Martin's.

Knoller, M. (2012, May 11). Obama touts marriage stance, fairness—Hollywood answers with $15M for campaign. Cbsnews.com. Retrieved from: http://www.cbsnews.com/8301-503544_162-57432357-503544/obama-touts-marriage-stance-fairness-hollywood-answers-with-$15m-for-campaign.

Koppel, N. (2011, August 25). On red-light cameras and the constitution. *Wall Street Journal*. Retrieved from: http://blogs.wsj.com/law/2011/08/25/on-red-light-cameras-and-the-constitution.

Krauthammer, C. (2009, August 7). A better plan for health-care reform. *Washington post*. Retrieved from: http://www.washingtonpost.com/wp-dyn/content/article/2009/08/06/AR2009080602933.html.

Kurtzleben, D. (2012, June 28). National security a crucial part of STEM discussion. *U.S. News & World Report*. Retrieved from: http://www.usnews.com/news/blogs/stem-education/2012/06/28/national-security-a-crucial-part-of-stem-discussion.

Lankshear, C., & Knobel, M. (2011). *New literacies*. Berkshire, UK: Open University Press.

Lapsley, D. K., & Power, F. C. (2005). *Character psychology and character education*. Notre Dame, IN: University of Notre Dame Press.

Lazarus, D. (2007, December 23). Best Buy kiosks not connected to Internet. *Los Angeles Times*. Retrieved from: http://www.latimes.com/business/la-fi-lazarus23dec23,1,5748783.column.

Lee, M. (1983). *A history of physical education and sports in the U.S.A.* New York: Wiley.

Levitz, J. (2011, April 26). Tea party heads to school. *Wall Street Journal.* Retrieved from: http://online.wsj.com/article/SB1000142405274 870433650457625954330385376.html.

Lewin, L. (2003). *Paving the way in reading and writing: Strategies and activities to support struggling students in grades 6-12.* San Francisco: Jossey-Bass.

Lewin, T. (2010, July 21). Many states adopt national standards for their schools. *New York Times.* Retrieved from: http://www.nytimes. com/2010/07/21/education/21standards.html.

Lewin, T. (2012, July 29). Senate committee report on for-profit colleges condemns costs and practices. *New York Times.* Retrieved from: http://www.nytimes.com/2012/07/30/education/harkin-report-condemns-for-profit-colleges.html.

Lichtenstein, B. (2012, September 8). A terrifying way to discipline children. *New York Times.* Retrieved from: http://www.nytimes.com/2012/09/09/opinion/sunday/a-terrifying-way-to-discipline-children.html.

Lieszkovszky, I. (2011, November 21). Some Ohio schools say computers don't belong in classrooms. State Impact. Retrieved from: http:// stateimpact.npr.org/ohio/2011/11/21/some-schools-say-computers-dont-belong-in-classrooms.

Lights, cameras, reaction: Resistance builds against red-light cameras. (2013, February 19). Nbcnews.com. Retrieved from: http://open-channel.nbcnews.com/_news/2013/02/19/17010355-lights-cameras-reaction-resistance-builds-against-red-light-cameras.

Lim, D. (2012, May 11). Giving chase to young love on the run. *New York Times.* Retrieved from: http://www.nytimes.com/2012/05/13/movies/wes-andersons-moonrise-kingdom-with-bill-murray.html.

Lim, E. T. (2008). *The anti-intellectual presidency: The decline of presidential rhetoric from George Washington to George W. Bush.* Oxford, UK: Oxford University Press.

Lopez, S. (2013, April 27). IPads in school: A toy or a tool? *Los Angeles Times.* Retrieved from: http://articles.latimes.com/2013/apr/27/local/la-me-0428-lopez-ipads-20130428.

Los Angeles teacher ratings. (2010). *Los Angeles Times* [local edition]. Retrieved from: http://projects.latimes.com/value-added.

Lowrey, A. (2012, January 6). Big study links good teachers to lasting gain. *New York Times*. Retrieved from: http://www.nytimes.com/2012/01/06/education/big-study-links-good-teachers-to-lasting-gain.html.

Lucchetti, A., & Philbin, B. (2012, August 8). Now, it is man vs. machine. *Wall Street Journal*. Retrieved from: http://online.wsj.com/article/SB10000872396390044399170457757719004911898O.html.

Luntz, F. I. (2007). *Words that work: It's not what you say, it's what people hear*. New York: Hyperion.

Luscombe, B. (2010, September 6). Do we need $75,000 a year to be happy? *Time*. Retrieved from: http://www.time.com/time/magazine/article/0,9171,2019628,00.html.

Lyons, W., & Drew, J. (2006). *Punishing schools: Fear and citizenship in American public education*. Ann Arbor: University of Michigan Press.

Maass, B. (2009, September 9). Denver lawyer wants to put ads on cop cars. Xdtalk.com. Retrieved from: http://www.xdtalk.com/forums/leo-talk/130113-ads-police-cars-what-do-you-think.html.

Mack, K. (2012, June 25). Emanuel seeks bids for speed-camera installation. *Chicago Tribune*. Retrieved from: http://articles.chicagotribune.com/2012-06-25/news/ct-met-speed-cameras-0626-20120626_1_speed-cameras-speed-camera-business-red-light-cameras.

Madison, L. (2012, November 27). Ahead of education summit, Jeb Bush stays mum about 2016. Cbsnews.com. Retrieved from: http://www.cbsnews.com/8301-34222_162-57554671-10391739/ahead-of-education-summit-jeb-bush-stays-mum-about-2016.

Maeroff, G. I. (1975, December 6). The return to fundamentals in the nation's schools. *New York Times*. Retrieved from: http://select.nytimes.com/gst/abstract.html?res=FA0C13F73D5C1A7493C4A91789D95F418785F9.

Maeroff, G. I. (1977, October 25). Competency tests backed by Califano. *New York Times*. Retrieved from: http://select.nytimes.com/gst/abstract.html?res=F40815F73D5D147A93C7AB178BD95F438785F9.

Maeroff, G. I. (1979, June 11). As Antioch College grows, so does its anxiety over finances, tradition and identity: Tradition of liberalism. *New York Times*. Retrieved from: http://select.nytimes.com/gst/abstract.html?res=F30D15F93E5D12728DDDA80994DE405B898BF1D3.

Manian, D. (2012). *HTML5 boilerplate web development*. Birmingham: Packt.

Margolick, D. (1993, December 17). Texas lawyers to vote on how far their ads can go. *New York Times*. Retrieved from: http://www.nytimes.com/1993/12/17/news/texas-lawyers-to-vote-on-how-far-their-ads-can-go.html.

Mattioli, D., & Fitzgerald, D. (2012, September 10). Kodak CFO leaves; more jobs cut. *Wall Street Journal*. Retrieved from: http://online.wsj.com/article/SB10000872396390444554704577643313359142858.html.

Mattioli, D., Spector, M., & Jones, A. (2012, August 10). Kodak patent bidding is tame. *Wall Street Journal*. Retrieved from: http://online.wsj.com/article/SB10000872396390443537404577581542972796710.html.

Matus, R. (2011, January 11). Florida schools ranked No. 5 in U.S., according to Education Week. *Tampa Bay Times*. Retrieved from: http://www.tampabay.com/news/education/k12/florida-schools-ranked-no-5-in-us-according-to-education-week/1144718.

McCall, J. (2011). *Gaming the past: Using video games to teach secondary history*. London: Routledge.

McClurg, T., & Brighty, M. (2004). *Targeted business management: A back to basics approach*. London: Spiro.

McCune, G. (2012, September 15). Chicago teachers to stage big rally amid hopes of end to strike. Reuters.com. Retrieved from: http://www.reuters.com/article/2012/09/15/us-usa-chicago-schools-idUS-BRE88D12E20120915.

McDermott, K. A. (2011). *High-stakes reform: The politics of educational accountability*. Washington, DC: Georgetown University Press.

Mead, G. H. (1934). *Mind, self and society from the standpoint of a social behaviorist*. Chicago: University of Chicago Press.

Medina, J. (2009, January 29). Debate on mayoral control of schools is renewed. *New York Times*. Retrieved from: http://www.nytimes.com/2009/01/30/education/30control.html.

Medina, J. (2013, March 3). National attention and cash in Los Angeles school vote. *New York Times*. Retrieved from: http://www.nytimes.com/2013/03/04/education/los-angeles-school-board-race-attracts-national-attention-and-money.html.

Merrow, J. (2011). The joys of educational jargon. *Huffington Post*. Retrieved from: http://www.huffingtonpost.com/john-merrow/the-joys-of-educational-j_b_853247.html.

Michaels, S., Shouse, A. W., & Schweingruber, H. A. (2008). *Ready, set, science: Putting research to work in K-8 science classrooms*. Washington, DC: National Academies Press.

Miracle, A. W., & Rees, C. R. (1994). *Lessons of the locker room: The myth of school sports*. Amherst, NY: Prometheus.

Mitchell, J. (1996). *Joe Gould's secret*. New York: Modern Library. (Original work published in 1964)

Monroe, B. J. (2004). *Crossing the digital divide: Race, writing, and technology in the classroom*. New York: Teachers College Press.

Moskin, J. (2012, March 13). I was a cookbook ghostwriter. *New York Times*. Retrieved from: http://www.nytimes.com/2012/03/14/dining/i-was-a-cookbook-ghostwriter.html.

Mosle, S. (2012, November 22). What should children read? *New York Times*. Retrieved from: http://opinionator.blogs.nytimes.com/2012/11/22/what-should-children-read.

Mowrer, R. R., & Klein, S. B. (2001). *Handbook of contemporary learning theories*. Mahwah, NJ: Erlbaum.

Murphy, T. (2011, August 29). STEM education—It's elementary. *U.S. News & World Report*. Retrieved from: http://www.usnews.com/news/articles/2011/08/29/stem-education--its-elementary.

Nagel, D. (2009, August 26). Federal grants aim to boost STEM equity. *The Journal*. Retrieved from: http://thejournal.com/articles/2009/08/26/federal-grants-aim-to-boost-stem-equity.aspx.

National Association for Sport and Physical Education. (2004). *Moving into the future: National standards for physical education*. Reston, VA: Author.

National Center for History in the Schools. (1996). *National standards for history*. Los Angeles: Author.

National Council of Teachers of Mathematics. (1989). *Curriculum and evaluation standards for school mathematics*. Reston, VA: Author.

National Council of Teachers of Mathematics. (2000). *Principles and standards for school mathematics*. Reston, VA: National Council of Teachers of Mathematics.

National Institutes of Health. (2012, November 30). What is the best way to teach children to read? *National Institute of Child Health and Human Development*. Retrieved from: http://www.nichd.nih.gov/health/topics/reading/conditioninfo/pages/teach.aspx.

National Research Council. (1996). *National science education standards: Observe, interact, change, learn*. Washington, DC: National Academy Press.

National Standards in Foreign Language Education Project. (1999). *Standards for foreign language learning in the 21st century*. Lawrence, KS: Author.

New York City Schools. (2013). Progress report. Nyc.gov. Retrieved from: http://schools.nyc.gov/Accountability/tools/report/default.htm.

Nissenbauma, H., & Walkerb, D. (1988). Will computers dehumanize education? A grounded approach to values at risk. *Technology in Society*. 20, 237–73.

Noah, T. (2012, June 15). Obama's economic speech: What's missing. *New Republic*. Retrieved from: http://www.tnr.com/blog/plank/104090/obamas-economic-speech-whats-missing.

Noddings, N. (2002). *Educating moral people: A caring alternative to character education*. New York: Teachers College Press.

Nucci, L. P., & Narváez, D. (2008). *Handbook of moral and character education*. New York: Routledge.

O'Connor, J. (2013, April 24). Corporal punishment will return to Marion County elementary schools. Stateimpact.npr.org. Retrieved from: http://stateimpact.npr.org/florida/2013/04/24/corporal-punishment-will-return-to-marion-county-elementary-schools.

Omer, S. (2012, September 11). Question at heart of Chicago strike: How do you measure teacher performance? Nbcnews.com. Retrieved from: http://usnews.nbcnews.com/_news/2012/09/11/13808109-question-at-heart-of-chicago-strike-how-do-you-measure-teacher-performance.

Oppenheimer, T. (2003). *The flickering mind: The false promise of technology in the classroom, and how learning can be saved*. New York: Random House.

Ortutay, B. (2012, July 27). Facebook shares sink to new low after 2Q results. Msn.com. Retrieved from: http://www.msnbc.msn.com/id/48352456/ns/technology_and_science-tech_and_gadgets.

Pace, E. (1992, June 11). Morris Kline, 84, math professor and critic of math teaching, dies. *New York Times*. Retrieved from: http://www.nytimes.com/1992/06/11/nyregion/morris-kline-84-math-professor-and-critic-of-math-teaching-dies.html.

Pareles, J. (1990, November 20). Wages of silence: Milli Vanilli loses a Grammy Award. *New York Times*. Retrieved from: http://www.nytimes.com/1990/11/20/arts/wages-of-silence-milli-vanilli-loses-a-grammy-award.html.

Parker-Pope, T. (2010, June 6). An ugly toll of technology: Impatience and forgetfulness. *New York Times*. Retrieved from: http://www.nytimes.com/2010/06/07/technology/07brainside.html.

Parmet, H. S. (1980). *Jack: The struggles of John F. Kennedy*. New York: Dial.

Pennington, B. (2013, May 11). Hidden threats to young athletes. *New York Times*. Retrieved from: http://www.nytimes.com/2013/05/12/sports/safety-advocates-focus-on-hidden-threats-to-young-athletes.html.

Perr, J. (2008, June 23). "Aware of the internet," computer non-user McCain touts eBay as recession cure. Crooksandliars.com. Retrieved from: http://crooksandliars.com/2008/06/24/aware-of-the-internet-computer-non-user-mccain-touts-ebay-as-recession-cure.

Peters, J. W. (2012, July 15). Latest word on the trail: I take it back. *New York Times*. Retrieved from: http://www.nytimes.com/2012/07/16/us/politics/latest-word-on-the-campaign-trail-i-take-it-back.html.

Peterson, P. E. (Ed.). (2006). *Choice and competition in American education*. Lanham, MD: Rowman & Littlefield.

Petri, A. (2012, May 31). The real joke of the John Edwards verdict. *Washington Post*. Retrieved from: http://www.washingtonpost.com/blogs/compost/post/the-real-joke-of-the-john-edwards-verdict/2012/05/31/gJQAsQr24U_blog.html.

Pflaum, W. D. (2004). *The technology fix: The promise and reality of computers in our schools*. Alexandria, VA: Association for Supervision and Curriculum Development.

Phillips, E. E. (2013, May 15). Schools rethink suspension. *Wall Street Journal*. Retrieved from: http://online.wsj.com/article/SB10001424127887323339820457848535313964153&8.html.

Picciano, A. G., & Spring, J. H. (2013). *The great American education-industrial complex: Ideology, technology, and profit*. New York: Routledge.

Postal, L. (2011, March 26). In Florida, teacher pay now tied to performance. *Los Angeles Times*. Retrieved from: http://www.latimes.com/news/nationworld/nation/la-na-teacher-merit-pay-20110326,0,5609667.story.

President Clinton: Announcing new steps to support charter schools. (2000, May 4). Nara.gov. Retrieved from: http://clinton3.nara.gov/WH/Work/050500.html.

Proffitt, B. (2011). *iPad for kids: Using the iPad to play and learn.* Boston: Course Technology.

Radin, M. J. (2013). *Boilerplate: The fine print, vanishing rights, and the rule of law.* Princeton, NJ: Princeton University Press.

Rado, R. (2010, August 9). Illinois textbook costs going up. *Chicago Tribune*. Retrieved from: http://articles.chicagotribune.com/2010-08-09/news/ct-met-textbook-cuts-20100808_1_textbook-costs-book-sale-u-46.

Raice, S., Das, A., & Chon, G. (2012, May 23). Inside fumbled Facebook offering. *Wall Street Journal*. Retrieved from: http://online.wsj.com/article/SB10001424052702304019404577420660698374718.html.

Ramsey, R. (2012, September 20). Focusing on education, with an eye on the voters. *New York Times*. Retrieved from: http://www.nytimes.com/2012/09/21/us/texas-politicians-focus-on-education-with-eye-on-voters.html.

Randall, D. (2012). States with corporal punishment in school. Familyeducation.com. Retrieved from: http://school.familyeducation.com/classroom-discipline/resource/38377.html.

Ravitch, D. (1998). The controversy over national history standards. *Bulletin of the American Academy of Arts and Sciences, 51* (3), 14–28.

Reilly, S., & Schachtman, T. R. (2009). *Conditioned taste aversion: Behavioral and neural processes.* Oxford, UK: Oxford University Press.

Resmovits, J. (2010, August 16). Taking schools into their own hands. *Wall Street Journal*. Retrieved from: http://online.wsj.com/article/SB10001424052748704268004575417301793522096.html.

Reyes, A. H. (2006). *Discipline, achievement, and race: Is zero tolerance the answer?* Lanham, MD: Rowman & Littlefield.

Rich, M. (2007, November 19). Study links drop in test scores to a decline in time spent reading. *New York Times*. Retrieved from: http://www.nytimes.com/2007/11/19/arts/19nea.html.

Richards, E. (2012, August 19). School districts explore performance-based pay models. *Journal Sentinel*. Retrieved from: http://www.json-line.com/news/education/school-districts-explore-performancebased-pay-models-186es4a-166708646.html.

Richtel, M. (2010, November 21). Growing up digital, wired for distraction. *New York Times*. Retrieved from: http://www.nytimes.com/2010/11/21/technology/21brain.html.

Richtel, M. (2011a, September 3). In classroom of future, stagnant scores. *New York Times*. Retrieved from: http://www.nytimes.com/2011/09/04/technology/technology-in-schools-faces-questions-on-value.html.

Richtel, M. (2011b, November 4). Silicon Valley wows educators, and woos them. *New York Times*. Retrieved from: http://www.nytimes.com/2011/11/05/technology/apple-woos-educators-with-trips-to-silicon-valley.html.

Ripley, A. (2010, January 1). What makes a great teacher? *Atlantic*. Retrieved from: http://www.theatlantic.com/magazine/archive/2010/01/what-makes-a-great-teacher/307841.

Rivera, S. (2013, February 28). What is the purpose of school? *National Education Policy Center*. Retrieved from: http://nepc.colorado.edu/blog/what-purpose-school.

Rosen, L. D., Carrier, M. L., & Cheever, N. A. (2010). *Rewired: Understanding the iGeneration and the way they learn*. New York: Palgrave Macmillan.

Rubin, J. (2012a, April 17). John Edwards downgrades haircut from $1,250 to $12.95. Styleite.com. Retrieved from: http://www.styleite.com/beauty/john-edwards-haircuts/#0.

Rubin, J. (2012b, June 14). Obama speech: 54 minutes to say nothing. *Washington Post*. Retrieved from: http://www.washingtonpost.com/blogs/right-turn/post/obama-speech-54-minutes-to-say-nothing/2012/06/14/gJQAIZw4cV_blog.html.

Ruiz, R. R. (2012, October 13). Florida governor wants funds to go to practical degrees. *New York Times*. Retrieved from: http://thechoice.blogs.nytimes.com/2011/10/13/rick-scott.

Ruschmann, P. (2006). *Tort reform*. Philadelphia: Chelsea House.

Sanchez, J., & Weigel, D. (2008, January 16). Who wrote Ron Paul's newsletters? Reason.com. Retrieved from: http://reason.com/archives/2008/01/16/who-wrote-ron-pauls-newsletter.

Sanders, T. (2011, December 10). Educators question use of grade-recovery programs. *Florida Times-Union*. Retrieved from: http://m.jacksonville.com/news/metro/2011-12-10/story/student-grade-recovery-increases-duval-teachers-question-its-message.

Santos, F., & Phillips, A. M. (2012, February 26). With release of teacher data, setback for union turns into a rallying cry. *New York Times*. Retrieved from: http://www.nytimes.com/2012/02/27/nyregion/teacher-ratings-produce-a-rallying-cry-for-the-union.html.

Saunders, B. J., & Goddard, C. (2010). *Physical punishment in childhood: The rights of the child*. West Sussex, UK: Wiley-Blackwell.

Sawchuk, S. (2012, March 23). Arne Duncan: Newspapers shouldn't publish teacher ratings. *Education Week*. Retrieved from: http://blogs.edweek.org/edweek/teacherbeat/2012/03/arne_duncan_newspapers_shouldn.html.

Scholastic launches new suite of learning tools. (2013, April 17). Digitalbookworld.com. Retrieved from: http://www.digitalbookworld.com/2013/scholastic-launches-new-suite-of-learning-tools.

School reform on the ballot. (2012, October 29). *Wall Street Journal*. Retrieved from: http://online.wsj.com/article/SB10001424052970204840504578086773381885236.html.

Schweber, N. (2012, August 8). At La Guardia, a smiling helper materializes, digitally. *New York Times*. Retrieved from: http://www.nytimes.com/2012/08/09/nyregion/la-guardias-digital-avatar-gives-passengers-airport-information.html.

Science, technology, engineering and mathematics (STEM) workforce division. (2012). National Defense Industrial Association. Retrieved from: http://www.ndia.org/divisions/divisions/stem/Pages/default.aspx.

Sciolino, E. (2012, June 20). The French still flock to bookstores. *New York Times*. Retrieved from: http://www.nytimes.com/2012/06/21/books/french-bookstores-are-still-prospering.html.

Scott, T. M., Anderson, C. M., & Alter, P. (2012). *Managing classroom behavior using positive behavior supports*. Boston: Pearson.

Shanks, A. (2012, March 5). Publicizing teacher evaluations draws criticism. Legislativegazette.com. Retrieved from: http://www.legislativegazette.com/Articles-Top-Stories-c-2012-03-05-81399.113122-Publicizing-teacher-evaluations-draws-criticism.html.

Shaywitz, S. E. (2003). *Overcoming dyslexia: A new and complete science-based program for reading problems at any level*. New York: Knopf.

Shea, C. (2012, May 23). Education and military rivalry: More closely tied than you think. *Wall Street Journal*. Retrieved from: http://blogs.wsj.com/ideas-market/2012/05/23/education-and-military-rivalry-more-closely-tied-than-you-think.

Shipps, D. (2006). *School reform, corporate style: Chicago, 1880–2000*. Lawrence: University Press of Kansas.

Should schools continue to use textbooks, why or why not? (2012, September 24). *Valley Morning Star*. Retrieved from: http://www.valleymorningstar.com/sie/fresh_ink/article_3f03f35c-0692-11e2-959d-0019bb30f31a.html.

Should schools embrace "bring your own device"? (2012, July 19). *NEA Today*. Retrieved from: http: //neatoday.org/2012/07/19/should-schools-embrace-bring-your-own-device.

Should students influence how much teachers get paid? (2013, April 17). *Guardian*. Retrieved from: http://www.guardian.co.uk/teacher-network/teacher-blog/2013/apr/17/teachers-performance-pay-students-influence.

Should we be paying students? (2011, October 13). *Learning Matters*. Retrieved from: http://learningmatters.tv/blog/web-series/discuss-should-we-be-paying-students/7769.

Silver, H. F., Strong, R. W., & Perini, M. J. (2000). *So each may learn: Integrating learning styles and multiple intelligences*. Alexandria, VA: Association for Supervision and Curriculum Development.

Simon, S. (2012, November 27). Jeb Bush's reputation as education reformer gets a second look. Nbcnews.com. Retrieved from: http://openchannel.nbcnews.com/_news/2012/11/27/15485391-jeb-bushs-reputation-as-education-reformer-gets-a-second-look?lite.

Singer, S. R., Hilton, M. L., & Schweingruber, H. A. (2006). *America's lab report: Investigations in high school science*. Washington, DC: National Academies Press.

Skinner, B. F. (1974). *About behaviorism*. New York: Knopf.

Smith, M. (2010, September 16). Perry says the state needs more tort reform. *Texas Tribune*. Retrieved from: http://www.texastribune.org/texas-politics/2010-texas-governors-race/perry-says-the-state-needs-more-tort-reform.

Smith, M. (2012, May 31). Trial lawyers' support of Republican candidates yields less than stellar results. *New York Times*. Retrieved from: http://www.nytimes.com/2012/06/01/us/texas-trial-lawyers-support-of-republicans-yields-mixed-results.html.

Smith, T. (2012, September 13). Teacher evaluation dispute echoes beyond Chicago. *National Public Radio*. Retrieved from: http://www.npr.org/2012/09/13/160247078/teacher-evaluation-dispute-echoes-beyond-chicago.

Sobel, D. (1990, August 20). B. F. Skinner, the champion of behaviorism, is dead at 86. *New York Times*. Retrieved from: http://www.nytimes.com/1990/08/20/obituaries/b-f-skinner-the-champion-of-behaviorism-is-dead-at-86.html.

Song, J. (2010, August 25). U.S. schools chief to push disclosure. *Los Angeles Times*. Retrieved from: http://www.latimes.com/news/local/teachers-investigation/la-me-teachers-teachers-arne-duncan,0,3470133.story.

Speck, R. (2012, October 8). Is it right for parents to take over schools? Ted.com. Retrieved from: http://www.ted.com/conversations/14262/is_it_right_for_parents_to_tak.html.

Spector, M., & Mattioli, D. (2012, January 5). Kodak teeters on the brink. *Wall Street Journal*. Retrieved from: http://online.wsj.com/article/SB10001424052970203471004577140841495542810.html.

Spector, M., Mattioli, D., & Brickley, P. (2012, January). Can bankruptcy filing save Kodak? *Wall Street Journal*. Retrieved from: http://online.wsj.com/article/SB10001424052970204555904577169920031456052.html.

Starr, L. (1998, January 12). Setting standards in our schools: What can we expect? Educationworld.com. Retrieved from: http://www.educationworld.com/a_admin/admin/admin042.shtml.

STEM Grants. (2012, March 7). Stemgrants.com. Retrieved from: http://stemgrants.com.

STEM schools—Best high schools. (2012). *U.S. News & World Report*. Retrieved from: http://www.usnews.com/education/best-high-schools/national-rankings/stem.

Stone, R. (2005). *Best classroom management practices for reaching all learners: What award-winning classroom teachers do*. Thousand Oaks, CA: Corwin.

Straubhaar, J. D., LaRose, R., & Davenport, L. (2013). *Media now: Understanding media, culture, and technology*. Boston, MA: Wadsworth.

Strauss, V. (2010, June 1). Chicago's teacher performance-based pay didn't work—New analysis. *Washington Post*. Retrieved from: http://voices.washingtonpost.com/answer-sheet/research/analysis-of-chicagos-teacher-p.html.

Strauss, V. (2012, July 27). Randi Weingarten calls for "new approach to unionism" and support for Obama. *Washington Post*. Retrieved from: http://www.washingtonpost.com/blogs/answer-sheet/post/randi-weingarten-calls-for-new-approach-to-unionism-and-support-for-obama/2012/07/27/gJQAqfJuDX_blog.html.

Stross, R. (2011, December 24). Publishers vs. libraries: An e-book tug of war. *New York Times*. Retrieved from: http://www.nytimes.com/2011/12/25/business/for-libraries-and-publishers-an-e-book-tug-of-war.html.

Stuhldreher, A. (2008, October 15). Pay to learn is working in New York. *Los Angeles Times*. Retrieved from: http://www.latimes.com/news/opinion/commentary/la-oe-stuhl15-2008oct15,0,5060228.story.

Sunderman, G. L. (2009). The federal role in education: From the Reagan to the Obama administration. Annenberg Institute. Retrieved from: http://annenberginstitute.org/VUE//summer09/Sunderman.php.

Sylvester, S. (2010, August 15). The benefits of tort reform in Texas. Tortreform.com. Retrieved from: http://www.tortreform.com/node/583.

Symposium on National Standards for Education in the Arts. (1994). *The vision for arts education in the 21st century: The ideas and ideals behind the development of the national standards for education in the arts*. Reston, VA: Music Educators National Conference.

Testing industry's big four. (2002). Pbs.org. Retrieved from: http://www.pbs.org/wgbh/pages/frontline/shows/schools/testing/companies.html.

Thomas, P. L. (2012, April 26). Politics and education don't mix. *Atlantic*. Retrieved from: http://www.theatlantic.com/national/archive/2012/04/politics-and-education-dont-mix/256303.

Thomsen, M. (2013, May 1). The case against grades. Slate.com. Retrieved from: http://www.slate.com/articles/double_x/doublex/2013/05/the_case_against_grades_they_lower_self_esteem_discourage_creativity_and.html.

Thurm, S., Raice, S., & Demos, T. (2012, July 27). Social-media stock frenzy fizzles. *Wall Street Journal*. Retrieved from: http://online.wsj.com/article/SB10000872396390443477104577553431459135876.html.

Tibken, S. (2012, January 17). Apple to give a lesson about textbooks. *Wall Street Journal*. Retrieved from: http://online.wsj.com/article/SB10001424052970203721704577159163902420548.html.

Tierney, J. (2012, December 11). For lesser crimes, rethinking life behind bars. *New York Times*. Retrieved from: http://www.nytimes.com/2012/12/12/science/mandatory-prison-sentences-face-growing-skepticism.html.

Todd, C., Murray, M., Brower, B., & Cucchiara, N. (2012, June 13). First thoughts: Running out the clock. Msnbc.msn.com. Retrieved from: http://firstread.msnbc.msn.com/_news/2012/06/13/12201432-first-thoughts-running-out-the-clock?lite.

Toppo, G. (2010, March 3). Teachers counter education reform ideas on tests, pay. *USA Today*. Retrieved from: http://usatoday30.usatoday.com/news/education/2010-03-03-teachersurvey03_st_N.htm.

Toppo, G. (2012, April 1). Common Core standards drive wedge in education circles. *USA Today*. Retrieved from: http://www.usatoday.com/news/education/story/2012-04-28/common-core-education/54583192/1.

Trachtenberg, J. A. (2011, April 11). Cheapest e-books upend the charts. *Wall Street Journal*. Retrieved from: http://online.wsj.com/article/SB10001424052748703838004576274813963609784.html.

Trachtenberg, J. A. (2012, July 1). Textbook case for expansion. *New York Times*. Retrieved from: http://online.wsj.com/article/SB1000142405270230483070457749654065071 0290.html.

Transformers 2. (2012, September 6). *Wall Street Journal*. Retrieved from: http://online.wsj.com/article/SB100008723963904436860045776352928615083 00.html.

Treen, D. (2012, July 6). Jacksonville attorney argues for ads in police cruisers. Jacksonville.com. Retrieved from: http://m.jacksonville.com/news/crime/2012-07-05/story/jacksonville-attorney-argues-ads-police-cruisers.

Trinkle, D. A., & Merriman, S. A. (2001). *History.edu: Essays on teaching with technology*. Armonk, NY: Sharpe.

Trousdale, W. B. (2006). *Military high schools in America*. Walnut Creek, CA: Left Coast.

Tugend, A. (2005, April 6). Public military academies put discipline in the schools. *New York Times*. Retrieved from: http://www.nytimes.com/2005/04/06/education/06academies.html.

Turner, D. (2010, April, 8). States push to pay teachers based on performance. *USA Today*. Retrieved from: http://usatoday30.usatoday.com/news/education/2010-04-08-teachers-pay_N.htm.

Turner, M. L. (2011). Ghostwriters now have a professional association to call their own! Associationofghostwriters.org. Retrieved from: http://www.associationofghostwriters.org/index.htm.

Turner, S. M. (2002). *Something to cry about: An argument against corporal punishment of children in Canada*. Waterloo, CA: Wilfrid Laurier University Press.

Union wins in Chicago. (2012, September 16). *Wall Street Journal*. Retrieved from: http://online.wsj.com/article/SB10000872396390444023704577651882966023046.html.

United States Committee on Science and Technology. (2007). *Federal STEM education programs: Hearings before the Subcommittee on Research and Science Education*. Washington, DC: Author.

United States Department of Education. (2012). *Teacher incentive fund*. Washington, DC: Author. Retrieved from: http://www2.ed.gov/programs/teacherincentive/index.html.

United States National Research Council. (2011). *Successful K–12 STEM education: Identifying effective approaches in science, technology, engineering, and mathematics*. Washington, DC: National Academies Press.

Vairo, P. D., Marcus, S., & Weiner, M. (2007). *Hot-button issues for teachers: What every educator needs to know about leadership, testing, textbooks, vouchers, and more*. Lanham, MD: Rowman & Littlefield.

Vamosi, R. (2011). *When gadgets betray us: The dark side of our infatuation with new technologies*. New York: Basic Books.

Van Orsdel, L. C., & Born, K. (2009, April 15). Reality bites: Periodicals price survey 2009. *Library Journal*. Retrieved from: http://www.libraryjournal.com/article/CA6651248.html.

Vanderkam, L. (2013, May 27). Can wealth really buy happiness? *USA Today*. Retrieved from: http://www.usatoday.com/story/opinion/2013/05/27/wealth-buy-happiness-oclumn/2364049.

Walch, T. (1996). *Parish school: American Catholic parochial education from colonial times to the present*. New York: Crossroad.

Walters, L. S. (1993, March 16). Clinton education policy pushes national standards. *Christian Science Monitor*. Retrieved from: http://www.csmonitor.com/1993/0316/16062.html.

Ward, D. (2013). Boilerplate. Politicaltheatre.net. Retrieved from: http://politicaltheatre.net/post/3277820330/boilerplate.

Watanabe, T. (2010, November 14). For L.A., possible lessons in D.C.'s controversial teacher evaluation system. *Los Angeles Times*. Retrieved from: http://articles.latimes.com/2010/nov/14/local/la-me-teachers-evals-20101114.

Watson, J. B. (1970). *Behaviorism*. New York: Norton. (Original work published in 1930)

Way, W. D. (2012, August 6). Texas state exams. *New York Times*. Retrieved from: http://www.nytimes.com/2012/08/07/opinion/texas-state-exams.html.

Weil, D. K. (2002). *School vouchers and privatization: A reference handbook*. Santa Barbara, CA: ABC-CLIO.

Weingarten, R. (2012, September 14). The struggle in Chicago. *Huffington Post*. Retrieved from: http://www.huffingtonpost.com/randi-weingarten/the-struggle-in-chicago_b_1885469.html.

Wells, H. (2012). *The fast and the furious: Drivers, speed cameras and control in a risk society*. Farnham, UK: Ashgate.

Western, B. (2006). *Punishment and inequality in America*. New York: Russell Sage.

What is the most important subject taught in school? (2007, December 22). Sciforums.com. Retrieved from: http://www.sciforums.com/showthread.php?75431-What-is-the-most-important-subject-taught-in-school.

Will, G. (2007, July 15). Farewell, Antioch. Townhall.com. Retrieved from: http://townhall.com/columnists/georgewill/2007/07/15/farewell,_antioch.

Winerip, M. (2012, June 10). Backtracking on Florida exams flunked by many, even an educator. *New York Times*. Retrieved from: http://www.nytimes.com/2012/06/11/education/florida-backtracks-on-standardized-state-tests.html.

Wood, D. B. (2002, October 3). Your ad here: Cop cars as the next billboards. *Christian Science Monitor*. Retrieved from: http://www.csmonitor.com/2002/1003/p01s01-ussc.html.

Wragg, E. C. (2004). *Performance pay for teachers: The views and experiences of heads and teachers*. London: RoutledgeFalmer.

Young, M. (Ed.). (2012). *For-profit education*. Detroit: Greenhaven.

Youniss, J., Convey, J. J., & McLellan, J. A. (Eds.). (2000). *The Catholic character of Catholic schools*. Notre Dame, IN: University of Notre Dame Press.

Zattoni, A., & Judge, W. Q. (Eds.). (2012). *Corporate governance and initial public offerings: An international perspective*. Cambridge, UK: Cambridge University Press.

Zernike, K. (2012, August 6). Christie signs bill overhauling job guarantees for teachers. *New York Times*. Retrieved from: http://www.nytimes.com/2012/08/07/nyregion/christie-signs-bill-overhauling-teacher-tenure.html.

Zimmerman, A. (2012a, April 11). Can retailers halt "showrooming"? *Wall Street Journal*. Retrieved from: http://online.wsj.com/article/SB10001424052702304587704577334370670243032.html.

Zimmerman, A. (2012b, August 30). Can electronics stores survive? *Wall Street Journal*. Retrieved from: http://online.wsj.com/article/SB10000872396390444772804577621581739401906.html.

ABOUT THE AUTHOR

Gerard Giordano is professor at the University of North Florida. He has written more than a dozen books, including *Solving Education's Problems Effectively*, *Cockeyed Education*, *Lopsided Schools*, *Capping Costs*, and *Teachers Go to Rehab*. All of these recent books were published by Rowman & Littlefield Education.

CPSIA information can be obtained at www.ICGtesting.com
Printed in the USA
BVOW08s0029240114

342840BV00002B/6/P